LIFE
After Death

Widows in Pennsylvania
1750–1850

In the series
AMERICAN CIVILIZATION
edited by Allen F. Davis

LIFE

After Death

Widows in Pennsylvania
1750–1850

LISA WILSON

TEMPLE UNIVERSITY PRESS

Philadelphia

Temple University Press, Philadelphia 19122
Copyright © 1992 by Temple University. All rights reserved
Published 1992
Printed in the United States of America

The paper used in this publication meets the minimum requirements of
American National Standard for Information Sciences—Permanence of
Paper for Printed Library Materials, ANSI Z39.48-1984 ∞

Library of Congress Cataloging-in-Publication Data

Wilson, Lisa, 1957–
    Life after death : widows in Pennsylvania, 1750–1850 / Lisa
Wilson.
        p.   cm.—(American civilization)
    Includes bibliographical references and index.
    ISBN 0-87722-883-3 (cloth)
        1. Widows—Pennsylvania—History—18th century. 2. Widows—
Pennsylvania—History—19th century. I. Title. II. Series.
HQ1058.5.U5W55   1992
305.48'9654—dc20   91-15289

To Alex

Acknowledgments

THIS BOOK benefited from the rich historical resources in the Philadelphia area and the people who manage these collections. Linda Stanley, Peter Parker, and Arlene Shaner guided me through the invaluable collections at the Historical Society of Pennsylvania. Ward Childs provided insights into the holdings of the Philadelphia City Archives. At the Chester County Historical Society, Rosemary B. Philips was particularly helpful in directing me through the Society's diverse genealogical sources. The staff of the Chester County Archives, particularly Laurie Rofini, went beyond the call of duty in contributing new sources and fresh ideas. Their enthusiasm and friendliness made my work easier and the final product immeasurably better.

The other resources of the Philadelphia area are of the human variety. Colonial historians abound and make the city a special place to develop intellectually. The Philadelphia Center for Early American Studies and, less formally, Michael Zuckerman's running forum and the Women's Working Group provided a place to try out new ideas and be exposed to the ongoing projects of other scholars. Of help also, during the final stages of my dissertation, were the Center's monetary resources.

Friends and colleagues have helped in a variety of ways to bring this project to fruition. These friendly mentors include colleagues at Temple University, the Philadelphia Center for Early American Studies, and Connecticut College. Some of the people who lent their time and support are John Andrew, Ava Baron, Herbert Ershkowitz, Ken Fones-Wolf, Marc Gallicchio, Shan Holt, Susan Klepp, Allan Kulikoff, Cindy Little, Susan Mackiewicz, Ric Northrup, Lucy Simler, Billy G. Smith, Merril Smith, Jean Soderlund, Marianne Wokeck, and Michael Zuckerman. In addition, I could not have accomplished the final stages of book revision without the childcare provided by Linda Ravenelle.

During my graduate work and since, I have profited above all from the advice of my dissertation advisor, P. M. G. Harris. He has demonstrated to me the careful, hard work necessary for "good" history. He always pushed me farther than I thought I could go and made me accomplish more than I thought I could. The hours he spent reading and rereading this book cannot be repaid, but I hope he will get some satisfaction out of the final product. His intellectual curiosity and integrity are a continuing source of inspiration.

Finally, Allen F. Davis and Janet Francendese helped me to improve both the organization and the language of the final manuscript. I hope the result conforms in some way to their exacting standards.

Parts of this book have been incorporated into presentations given at the Berkshire Conference on Women, the

Philadelphia Center for Early American Studies seminar, and the annual meeting of the Organization of American Historians. Chapter 4 appeared in slightly different form in the *William and Mary Quarterly.*

Contents

LIFE
After Death

Widows in Pennsylvania
1750–1850

Introduction

AT THE end of the twentieth century, political, religious, and social leaders lament the decline of the American family. Part of this perceived decay is due to the proliferation of "broken homes," many headed by women struggling to raise their children and support their families alone. This change in the landscape of familial relationships seems particularly disturbing to critics when measured against the blissful domestic world of the American past. This popular view, however, bears little resemblance to historical fact. Families were unstable and often female-headed prior to the late twentieth century. Death rather than divorce was the culprit. When families suffered the loss of a father and husband, the woman left behind, then as now, had to juggle financial and family responsibilities.[1] The *ideal* of a two-parent household links us to the past, as does the *reality* of many husbandless women coping with the challenges of life alone.

In early nineteenth-century Philadelphia, about 10 percent of the adult female population were widows. Half of the women who married became widows at some point in their lives, usually in their late forties. A widow commonly remained alone for almost fifteen years before her own death or remarriage. Most (more than 80 percent) never took the marriage vows again.[2] Among women who marry today, about 75 percent can expect to lose their husbands through death and to be about seventy years of age when widowed. The modern widow will be alone for almost twenty years. As in early America, most (66 percent) never marry again.[3] Widowhood is and was a common, long-term experience.

Widows in early Pennsylvania, like single mothers in the twentieth century, struggled to keep their families intact. They had an added handicap, however, in the prevailing ideology of proper female behavior. The ideal family, particularly among the middle class, was a gender-segregated institution.[4] Within this institution there were "separate spheres" of activity for men and women. Women worked in the domestic world, and men labored in the more public world of business. Within the female "sphere," women found some power in social and religious activities, in their ability to limit family size, and in the increasingly important role of motherhood.[5] Nonetheless, the worlds of men and women were distinct.

Given this prescriptive reality, the abilities of widowed women to provide economic stability for their families were remarkable. They went beyond picking up a husband's responsibilities.[6] Some widows excelled in their role as family provider. Carrying on business activities outside the home challenged prevailing ideas of femininity, and yet for a widow this concern, if it emerged at all, was secondary to the often pressing needs of her family. Like her twentieth-century counterpart, she worked to mend her broken home.

Writing in the early nineteenth century, Elizabeth Willing Powel, widow of the former mayor of Philadelphia, Samuel Powel, offered advice to her niece on the occasion of her marriage.

> To fix the variable Heart of Man to fan & keep alive that Affection by w<u>h</u>, alone, a woman can hope to preserve her Empire with a Man of Sense & Sensibility requires many Sacrifices great Dignity of Conduct without assuming, greater condesention in Trifles, a scrupulous Adherence to the Principles of Virtue & Integrity, a Chastity of Manners the nicest Delicacy of Conversation & Behavior even in the most private Hours, & an unbounded Confidence in the Honor & conjugal Fidelity of the Man on whose supreme Will you must eventually rest all your hopes of Happiness in this World. Sweetness of Temper, Patience, an accurate Degree of personal Neatness, with a proper Attention to domestic Comforts have more fascinating Charms in the Eyes of Men than the most brilliant & showy Talents unaccompanied by these engaging feminine Qualities. . . . Nature & Custom seems to have destined us for the more endearing & private & the Men for the more active & busy Walks of Life.[7]

Expressing thoughts undoubtedly gleaned from advice books and from her own sense of a woman's proper place, the Widow Powel echoed familiar cultural tenets. Whereas a man's world was "active & busy," a woman's sphere was domestic and "private," her happiness depending on her proper use of her "feminine Qualities" within the constraints determined by the "supreme Will" of a man.

The way the Widow Powel lived out these notions, however, demonstrates the difficult and complex nature of these "separate spheres."[8] While counseling her niece on the virtues of femininity, she carefully attended to her

land investments, using her extensive knowledge of stock
and land values to augment her own fortune as well as that
of her favorite nephew and adopted son, John Hare Powel.

In an 1809 letter to her surrogate son, she discussed the
value of her homestead in relation to a parcel he was
considering, and the problems of finding good tenants to
work the land.

> The Land and situation of Powelton renders it at least three
> times ~~more~~ as valuable, both as a Farm or as an object of
> revenue by letting lots on the various Roads by which the
> estate is bounded. Even the publick Road now contemplated
> will greatly enhance the value of my purchase of Guier,—
> which I now call Westland.

She well understood that the value of her land would be
increased through judicious exploitation. Replacing the
hapless Andrew McConnel, who "paid the Rent with punc-
tuality" and was "a very honest civil industrious Man;—
but devoid of the necessary knowledge to apply his industry beneficially," she offered the position at "a very low
rent to a Man of good character said to be an excellent
Farmer Garderner, and Fruiterer," provided he "put on the
Land One Hundred loads of Manure per Annum."[9]

A shrewd investor, Elizabeth Powel shed all her stock
in the Bank of the United States before the Congress failed
to renew the bank's charter in 1811. Beyond demonstrating
that she understood and functioned well in the male sphere
of business, the Widow Powel's financial maneuvering
showed little deference to male authority, again in direct
contradiction to the advice extended to her niece. She
informed her nephew: "Although my present communication may appear to you ungracious. Yet candour and a sense

of propriety impels me to make it. I have contrary to your advice; but in conformity with my own judgement and wishes after having reflected seriously on the subject sold all my United States Bank Stock." She went on to mention that her lawyer's advice "was very similar to that you gave."[10]

The rhetoric regarding female conduct bears little resemblance to the actual behavior of this widowed woman in early southeastern Pennsylvania. That is not to say, however, that Elizabeth Powel, and widows more generally, unwittingly or hypocritically violated cultural prescriptions. When proper femininity stood in the way of providing for herself and her family, cultural prescription was quietly put aside. Using her unfeminine skills in the public world of men allowed a widow to meet her family obligations. Widows' conduct reflects a necessary and sometimes seemingly contradictory layering of gender roles and family needs. The result is a whole larger than the parts, complex and yet completely compatible within the confines of an individual woman's life.

The lives of widows like Elizabeth Powel suggest an answer to the apparent enigma of separate spheres: Their world revolved around the family rather than issues of gender. Certainly gender definitions are part of family life; however, these women regarded their role as defined primarily within the context of the family. Issues of financial or legal power, of what could be deemed proper female behavior, faded in comparison with the overall priority of family survival after the loss of a father and husband. Adding this family focus to the concept of separate spheres makes the picture less dichotomous, and closer to a realistic representation of how these women viewed themselves and their lives. The core of their identity as women resided not solely in the home, but in the people who inhabited that domestic world—the family.

This study focuses on the crucial period of the late eighteenth and early nineteenth centuries.[11] The late eighteenth century saw the creation and development of a new nation. Industrialization began in cities like Philadelphia by the mid-nineteenth century. Many changes in American private life were observed during this period, including an increase in affection within the family. How did the lives of women develop in the context of such political, economic, and social changes?

Southeastern Pennsylvania then had a diverse population living in a mixed urban and rural environment. Religious toleration, a hallmark of William Penn's colony, encouraged members of numerous religious groups to migrate to the area. Similarly, the fertile land and booming economy of the region drew travelers and emigrants from many countries. As a result, Pennsylvania contained a broad cross-section of early American society by the late eighteenth century. Philadelphia and Chester counties clearly experienced many of the changes endemic to early America in a unique milieu of heterogeneity.

Between 1750 and 1850, Philadelphia County evolved from a mixed urban and rural environment to a large and expanding city. The population exploded from 14,330 in 1750 to 408,762 in 1850.[12] In the eighteenth century, the people of the city were primarily of English Quaker, Scots-Irish, and German stock.[13] By 1860 the population was 30 percent foreign-born, primarily Irish and German.[14]

Before the Revolution, this bustling seaport housed artisans and shopkeepers who often combined work space and domestic space.[15] By the mid-nineteenth century, however, the factory system had begun to take hold.[16] The artisan found his way of life permanently altered. The factory owner dictated production time, eradicating the more relaxed pace of the colonial artisan. The craftsman even lost the satisfaction of seeing the finished product because he produced only a part of the whole.[17]

Working away from home also altered family life. Husband and wife worked side by side in the corporate household of the preindustrial city. He would make the products, although a craftsman's wife and children could aid him in this process, and she would sell them. The family was a unit of production as well as consumption.[18] With the advent of industrialization, this integration of family and work began to change. The home, in fact, became a haven from the outside world of industry, at least among the white middle class.

The concentration of wealth, always part of this urban economy, became more pronounced: The poor became poorer and the rich became richer.[19] The merchants of Philadelphia particularly benefited from the new economic order as their high-risk ventures netted hefty profits.[20] On the lower end of the social scale, as the problems of urban poverty grew, institutions to house unfortunates were erected. First the Quakers and later the city government took on the job of constructing and maintaining an almshouse and a hospital to service the indigent.[21] The city became a magnet for those seeking opportunity on either the lofty plain of merchandising or the meaner level of mere subsistence. By 1850, Philadelphia had begun its course of urban and industrial expansion.

Chester County—on the border of this urban center—also grew between 1750 and 1850, but remained primarily a farming area. In 1789, part of the county was split off to form Delaware County, although both retained a rural cast. Estimates for the county population in 1750 are unreliable. In 1790, the year of the first U.S. census, the inhabitants of Chester County numbered 27,937. In 1850, this essentially rural community had grown to 66,438.[22] The people of Chester County came primarily from England, with a significant population of Scots-Irish and a few Germans and Welsh taking up residence in the fertile farm land as well. Those of English ancestry became more dominant over time as land became scarce and new arrivals looked for better opportunities to the west.[23]

The economy of this farming area relied on wheat for export along with some livestock and cheese consumed by the inhabitants of nearby Philadelphia.[24] This was the hinterland of Philadelphia. As a major exporter of wheat, the city depended on surrounding rural counties to supply this crop.[25] As time went on, the work of women on the farm, particularly the production of butter, became another important ingredient of the county's trade.[26]

Many farmers combined agricultural work with a trade or craft. Lucy Simler has discovered that a thorough examination of the personal possessions of a yeoman often reveals a loom or carpenter's tools, indicating a second occupation. This was far from a subsistence rural community. These farmer-artisans were market-minded small businessmen.[27]

Regardless of this profit-oriented perspective, yeomen in Chester County made their economic decisions within the context of the household. Mary Schweitzer, who studied this economic arrangement for an earlier period in the county's history, describes the household as a unit of both production and consumption.[28] For the late eighteenth and early nineteenth centuries, this characterization still seems appropriate. The family business was the farm, and everyone in the family worked to make this business successful. The jobs may have varied among family members, but everyone's contribution was crucial.

Compared with Philadelphia, Chester County's economic resources were more evenly divided among households. Overall, financial well-being was on the rise.[29] As the community grew, a network of small towns appeared, and there was a higher concentration of material resources among the wealthy by 1850.[30] The county as a whole, however, remained predominantly rural.

Chester and Philadelphia counties between 1750 and 1850 provide a backdrop against which many kinds of widows can be observed in different and changing contexts during a pivotal time in women's history. The first four chapters address issues of womanhood through the prism of widowhood, and in particular the abilities and priorities of widows and the contradictions and difficulties widowed women present for the concept of separate spheres. The last chapter tries to account for these apparent contradictions through an examination of the family's reaction to the loss of a husband and father. The Conclusion makes a case for the importance of the family perspective in assembling the puzzle of gender-based descriptions of women's lives.

1

"My Widowed State"

Writing to a friend shortly after the death of her beloved husband, John, in 1841, Sarah Grubb of Chester County commented, "Now I may tell thee that, since my J.G.'s removal to his eternal home, I am sensible continually of my widowed state."[1] Similarly, Deborah Norris Logan of Philadelphia remarked in her diary after death ended her forty-year marriage to George Logan, "My heart is sore, and wounded, and widowed."[2] Being widowed, they were aware of a personal sorrow as well as a bond with other mourning women. The death of a husband usually led to a period of mourning and psychological adjustment as the widow faced an array of challenges.[3] Widowhood was a common experience, and as such it reinforced women's reliance on each other; solidarity with other widowed women was one way of easing the transition from wife to widow.[4]

In the mid-nineteenth century, the public display of mourning became more acceptable, particularly for widows. This change has been linked to increasing sentimentality in the culture as a whole and the arrival of the Industrial Revolution,[5] but whatever its source, it is clear

11

that at this time widows began to dress distinctively for a period that might last for two years. As their mourning drew to an end, their dress, initially black, slowly brightened to shades of violet. Many women also wore a face veil.[6] In such a costume a woman announced her bereavement wherever she went, but she did not go abroad much. The proper widow curtailed her activities, remaining in the house except to attend church for the first month, and absenting herself from social events until the second year of her bereavement, when she was still expected to appear in her widow's weeds.[7] The widow's garb was a reminder of men's mortality and an advertisement of her status as a newly single woman.[8] It is small wonder that widows had a heightened awareness of their social condition.

On the other hand, the nineteenth-century widow's emotional response to her loss was little different from that of women in other eras. Widowhood clearly meant loneliness for a woman accustomed to sharing her life. Sarah Lynes Grubb was a Quaker minister who outlived her husband by only one year. She wrote to a friend about her feeling of isolation: "I feel stripped and lonely: missing my loved companion much, with whom I travelled so long in the path of life."[9] Sarah Clayton stated her feelings less directly in a letter to her niece in 1845: "You must My dear Anna think me very tedious—but you will I hope excuse me I am alone and when writing to a friend I can imagin them present & you know what my tongue has been—"[10] She craved companionship but feared imposing on her niece. Isolated and lonely, the widow searched for a way to replace the psychological support that her husband had provided.

Memories of happier times evoked, at least temporarily, a world in which the bereaved woman could forget her loneliness. In her book on modern widowhood, Helena Znaniecka Lopata observes that widows tend to sanctify their husband's memory, concentrating on the positive aspects of their lives together.[11] Sarah Lynes Grubb dwelt on the happiness of her marriage in a letter to a friend, making only slight mention of the senility that had claimed her husband before his death: "Although his mental powers were giving way in some degree, through the infirmities of age, yet I loved to be near him, and assist him what I could."[12] His condition may have caused her anxiety and even, perhaps, resentment as she played the role of nurse; but after his death, the memory became a positive one. Deborah Norris Logan tortured herself repeatedly with thoughts of her former happiness with George.

> At home and without company—and under depression of Spirits, a tender and afflicting remembrance, of my own best-loved and honoured friend filling my heart, heightened by meeting with one of his Letters in a Drawer where it accidentally had been left. My Soul is cloathed with mourning.[13]

The glorified memory of an idyllic marriage was bittersweet. The thought of past happiness was a comfort only until compared with the present of loneliness and despair.

Depression was common, in some instances lasting for years. Letters and diaries testify that, stripped of the role of wife, many widows felt their sense of purpose slip away. Deborah Norris Logan endured a kind of cyclical depression that lasted, though with diminishing intensity, until her own death eighteen years after her husband's.[14] A literate and highly educated woman, she recorded her inner thoughts throughout the period of her widowhood, from 1821 to 1839, in a diary that documents her lengthy and recurrent battle with depression. Her marriage had been long and happy. She described the death of her beloved George as a "Rupture [that] . . . violently severed and broke the texture of my happiness."[15] For days at a time, low spirits overwhelmed her. Sometimes her dark mood coincided with the anniversary of an event, such as her dead husband's birthday or the day of their wedding; at other times, her mood followed no discernible pattern. Typical of these periods were diary entries such as: "Third day passed in this low state of mind."[16] Her pain remained acute years after George's death. Three years into her widowhood she wrote, "The loss of my ever loved and honored husband, with that of the inestimable value of his kindness and affection to me, has sunk deep and fresh as if it had but just occurred."[17] She described herself as being "naturally light & cheerful, and not usually depressed without a cause,"[18] but little trace of this cheerful personality was evident for the duration of her widowhood.

Expressing a common sentiment, Deborah Norris Logan stated in her diary shortly after her husband's death, "I feel that I am but of little consequence to anyone and he who loved and valued me most is gone from it [the world] forever."[19] Without the role of wife, the widow had to extract her sense of purpose from other facets of her life. Margaret Murphy Craig, a widow from 1807 until 1814, wrote to her cousin in Belfast describing her efforts to do so: "In short if I am not happy myself I have at least the satisfaction to see all around me so and to be able to contribute in many ways to the comfort of those I love, which is all the Happiness I ever expect to Enjoy."[20] Sarah Clayton measured her usefulness to her children and herself in terms of the amount of business she transacted in her store on North 8th Street in Philadelphia. After eight years of widowhood, she wrote to her son in 1840: "It has been gratefying to stand usefull among my children, but I feel now and have done for sometime that my use to them weakens with my lack of business."[21]

Other women, less constructively, dwelled on their husband's death as well as on the possibility of their own.[22] Deep mourning and depression led, on occasion, to despair and a desire for release from emotional pain through death. Deborah Norris Logan regarded the possibility of death "as a subject of joy."[23] Margaret Shippen Arnold, the former Peggy Shippen and the widow of Benedict Arnold, wrote to her family of her morbid fascination with death.

> But indeed [death] itself had nearly been the consequences of the dispairing state to which I was reduced; for at our period, when I viewed everything through a false medium; —I fancied that anything but the sacrifice of my life could benefit my Children; for that my wretchedness embittered every moment of their lives;—and dreadful to say, I was many times on the point of making this sacrifice.[24]

The death of her closest companion heightened Deborah Norris Logan's awareness of the inevitability of her own demise, and she seems to have thought about it a great deal. She described herself as feeling like a "ship wrecked mariner, who has survived the storm in which he lost his companions, and sitting disconsolate on the shore reflecting on their fate and the means by which it might have been averted, regardless of the surge which is just ready to Sweep him into the same Gulph where they lie."[25] She developed a preoccupation with her husband's grave, located on her estate at Stenton, and she spent a good deal of time landscaping the site and directing the construction of a wall. In discussing the terms of a proposed will, her first thoughts were for the preservation of this fledgling family graveyard. Her ardent desire was that her grave "be at the site of his, to the left, and a small marble stone with our names and dates at the head of each Grave."[26]

The emotional stress of widowhood had its physical manifestations as well. Margaret Shippen Arnold told her father that her initial reaction to Benedict's long-expected death was "dejection, in the extreme . . . then as irritation not to be described." The numerous doctors she consulted prescribed everything from stimulants to opium.

> This was treated as wholly nervous; and hot, stimulating things given me, which were highly improper; as upon a consultation with a Physician of iminence, . . . he assures me that though my complaints are in a degree mental, they are greatly connected with those of the body, and have been produced by fulness of blood in the head, added to grief, loss of rest, and great anxiety of mind.[27]

Two years later she herself was dead.

Some lonely people use imagined or real illness as a method of extracting sympathy and concern from relatives and friends. Margaret Murphy Craig indulged in this type of emotional manipulation. A clandestine correspondence sprang up between Mrs. Craig and her future son-in-law, Nicholas Biddle, during his courtship of her daughter Jane. Typical of her efforts to draw sympathetic attention from him is a letter she wrote while under the influence of opium.

> I . . . wrote at a moment when it would have been a great task for me to write to any one else, which is pretty much my

situation at this moment as I have a head full of opium and a
body much fatigued, but while the heart is free and still alive
to hope I will not complain.[28]

The letter had the desired effect. Nicholas wrote, "Oh! my
darling friend you made me feel like a criminal at the idea
of having received a letter from you when you had 'a head
full of opium and a body much fatigued.' "[29]

Nicholas eventually tired of his future mother-in-law's
chronic illness and apparently accused her of enjoying the
attention she received when sick. She was indignant.

If this would not be too late for the Post I would finish with a
long scolding for something you said to me in one of your late
letters—is it possible then you think me such a selfish wretch
as to confine my self in my room merely for the sake of
indulging in retirement while my presence is really necessary
to those I so dearly love! Oh! Nicholas how little you know
me yet! but the time is coming when you will know me better
and so I forgive you.[30]

Desiring to stay in her good graces, Nicholas apologized in
his next letter, claiming that she "sadly misunderstood me
in supposing your retirement voluntary."[31] From this exchange it is unclear whether Nicholas actually accused
Mrs. Craig of reveling in imaginary illnesses or whether
she was overly sensitive on this issue. Either way, however,
Margaret Murphy Craig used her state of health to elicit
sympathy from the still eager-to-please Nicholas.

She interacted in a similar if more clearly manipulative
way with her son James. When James failed to write as
often as she liked, her expression of displeasure was
couched in terms of her delicate health. On receiving a

long-awaited letter, the Widow Craig claimed, "I was so overjoyed to see your hand I could scarcely break the seal, and I was unwell for half an hour after, let this prove to you how Dearly I love you and how much frequently hearing from you relates to my happiness."[32] In like fashion, James complained, "I see you are recovering your health my Dear Mother for, as I observed to you often before your convalescence is Generally accompanied by a strain of invective & abuse upon your poor son."[33] Clearly the Widow Craig's health was intertwined with her desire to control the behavior of those around her and extract the sympathy she thought she deserved.

Widows became resigned to widowhood in various ways. Sarah Clayton described to her niece a recent move to a new home: "But I moved here determind to be as happy as prospects would allow and when that resolve is only determind on I think many of the humane famialy might be more happy than they are—"[34] She reveals herself as a firm-willed woman who relied on strength of character to overcome problems and was impatient with those incapable of drawing on similar reserves. Some two years later, still resolved to accept her condition, she wrote to her niece, "I will strive to bear as I have through life my allotted portion of trials with firmness."[35] Statements of this sort helped to reinforce her determination as much as they conveyed information about her state of mind to an interested correspondent. Somewhat less firm, Deborah Norris Logan scolded herself for allowing routine problems—in this instance, with servants—to put her in a bad humor: "I have to check myself whenever I feel in this discontented mood and acknowledge I have much more to be thankful for, than discontented of."[36] She was less successful in dispelling her melancholy preoccupation with her departed husband. A widowed friend suggested that Margaret Murphy Craig dwell on the remaining sources of happiness in her life rather than her loss. "I sincerely hope the healing hand of time will dispose a mind like yours, to the enjoyment of the many blessings still left you."[37] In the end, resignation to the fact of widowhood remained difficult.

Religion gave some widows emotional solace. Exiled from the family she loved because of her infamous husband's treason, Margaret Shippen Arnold faced her widowhood in England. Her religion helped her deal with her crisis: "I have gone through many painful and distressing scenes, which had nearly overpower'd me; but I am now, thanks to the goodness of God, enabled to bear the great change in my situation with fortitude."[38] Sarah Lynes Grubb, a Quaker minister, felt that her religion provided a way to understand and account for her loss: "I am always sorrowful, yet rejoicing at his being fixed in his happy mansion, and that he knows nothing of my mourning as a dove."[39] That her husband enjoyed the unearthly pleasures of the afterlife was comfort enough. "My mind is consoled in contemplating the felicity of one almost dearer to me than myself, and that felicity uninterrupted for evermore."[40] Religion had been an integral part of their lives before widowhood, and long-held conviction made the death of a spouse easier to bear.

The love of her children could provide a focus and direction similar to the love of God. Many saw their offspring as their last source of happiness in this life. Deborah Norris Logan lamented, "Oh! how the pleasures and satisfactions of life recede from me. Quiet and Retirement and the affection of my children . . . is now almost all I want [desire crossed out above want]."[41] Sarah Clayton wrote to her daughter-in-law while on a trip, "I have been very happy on—this visit only as my thoughts dwell on what is always most dear, *my Children*."[42] Margaret Shippen Arnold, in a letter to her father, resolved "to be thankful for the blessings yet left me; —among the greatest of which is the uncommon excellence of my Children."[43] For these women, children served not only as a living memory of the husband they had lost, but also as an incentive to survive their misfortune and look to the future.

Having time to herself provided comfort and a break from new familial responsibilities. Deborah Norris Logan, rising before the rest of the household, usually wrote in her diary and pursued her other intellectual projects in the pre-dawn calm. "To me no way of life is so safe and so happy as solitude and retirement and that *by myself* (with occasional breaks of the call of friendship and social duties) I am happier and better contented with myself than I am in society."[44] Her description of her solitude as "safe" demonstrates her desire to shield herself from another heartbreaking death through self-reliance. She felt some anxiety, however, that her retreat from the world and desire for privacy might interfere with her social obligations.

This same sense of guilt plagued those widows who used travel to extract private time from occasionally reluctant families. Anne Emlen Mifflin felt obligated, as a Quaker minister, to fulfill a more public calling than raising her two young children, Samuel and Lemuel. Her mother cared for the boys while the Widow Mifflin made her proselytizing journeys. After setting out for Lancaster in 1813, she wrote to her mother about her ambivalence over leaving Samuel, who had apparently been feeling ill.

> Poor dear Samuel, under his tryed State, my mind was almost constantly with him in sympathy the day after setting out.

. . . Altho' I felt very dull for a day or two after leaving home—
yet have found my strength and appetite to improve, and have
been more released from the load of exercise attending my
affairs at home.[45]

Sarah Clayton also felt guilty about leaving home but
savored her temporary release from domestic concerns.
"Everything around me is pleasant & delightfull but still
my thoughts hover around home . . . I hope Elizabeth [a
servant] does her best if so I am sure if you are well you are
comfortable."[46] She acknowledged the pleasure she found
in solitude while on a visit to relatives on the eastern shore
of Maryland. "I finde quiet agrees with me & have had it
quite to my gratification once I have been down to Maryland."[47] Solitude of this sort could be regenerating, not a
sign of depression; it gave the widow an opportunity for
reflection as well as a respite from the household responsibilities she was now shouldering alone.

The universality of the process of resolution and adjustment to life alone is reflected in the affinity widows had
for women in similar circumstances. Deborah Norris Logan demonstrated her empathy in her frequent visits to
widowed friends. She dined at Mary Jones's home in Merion
soon after George's death. Her host was "the widow of
Jonathan Jones, whose death occurring just about the same
time that my husbands did, we have felt a very near
sympathy with each other."[48] In the spring of 1826, she
visited Polly Griffitts and Sally Longstreth. They spent the
afternoon discussing "their departed husband's in terms of
the tenderest affection." Deborah Norris Logan remarked
on that day, "I felt satisfied with going to these houses of
mourning."[49] An entry concerning Hannah Chancellor's

visit to the Logan home illustrated the same sense of solidarity among widows: "She has known what it is to lose an affectionate and good husband herself and has felt her loss deeply."[50]

References to other widows in the Widow Logan's diary allude to the responsibilities of widowhood as well as the emotional trauma. Problems were economic and parental. Deborah Norris Logan admired "poor Sally Logan" for "her spirit contemplating trying to do something to maintain herself and educate her poor little children."[51] Sally Longstreth's problems followed the same pattern. She was "left with 7 young children to educate—and, I am fearful, very small means, after her husbands debts are paid."[52] These widows had to handle financial and familial duties while trying to cope with the psychological repercussions of their loss.

Some went beyond empathy by providing economic support for poor widows through their wills. To achieve this, they left a small sum to their churches, or to an organization such as the Indigent Widows' and Single Women's Society of Philadelphia, to dispense among the most deserving. Some wished specifically to help widows with whom they had something in common. For example, Mary Bell helped widows of seafaring men through a contribution to the Society for the Relief of Poor and Distressed Masters of Ships, Their Widows and Children in memory of her late husband, Captain Thomas Bell.[53] Elizabeth Armitt left a legacy to her church to distribute among widows of her faith.[54] Through their wills, these widows left a permanent record of their desire to limit the hardships of other bereaved women.

Although each widow had to manage her own way, bereaved women entered a community of feeling that transcended social stratum, period in history, and place of residence. The "widowed state" was one of adjustment to loneliness as well as a new range of responsibilities. With a husband's death, a widow was immediately beset by legal, financial, and family problems. A woman became involved in matters of property and dealings with lawyers and judges in the often prolonged legal battle to settle her husband's estate; she was now responsible for providing food and shelter for her family in addition to bringing up children. How a widow handled these responsibilities in the midst of her grief and psychological adjustment tells us much about the inner resources and capabilities women brought to the challenges of widowhood.

2

Settling the Estate

Life is Short and uncertain. Death is the reverse and
every one ought to be prepared for it.
—*Garvin Hamilton, will proved in Philadelphia,*
  9 November 1830

In the usual rendering, a widow confronted with late
eighteenth- and early nineteenth-century Pennsylvania inheritance law and procedure had little control over the way
her husband's estate was settled, and she came away with
little property once creditors took their share.[1] This was in
fact the experience of some women, and seems to be the
only outcome possible under the harsh provisions of the
state's early inheritance law.

The law could, however, be circumvented legally or
extralegally. Marriage contracts and other devices had long
been used to soften the common law,[2] and widows also
had recourse to other methods, some less savory, to ensure
a larger inheritance. Moreover, individuals and courts executed inheritance law rather flexibly. Many people, particularly those with few possessions, never bothered with the
legalities of probate and intestate proceedings at all.[3] In

short, the reality of estate settlement was less severe for the widow than a simple reading of the law might indicate.

This chapter focuses on the settlement process to discover widow's strategies for obtaining power and to understand what power meant to them. Did they feel confined and powerless if not made sole executor and given a fee simple (or unrestricted) right to their entire inheritance?[4] Or did a widow consider herself an active and effective participant in the settlement process even without executorship or fee simple privileges? Certainly, married women, frequently in conjunction with their husbands, successfully sought ways to use—or even exploit—the legal system to ease their transition to widowhood.

With a few notable exceptions, Pennsylvania's inheritance law in the period between 1750 and 1850 was similar to that of other colonies or states. As in most of America, whether or not a Pennsylvania man left a will determined how his estate was settled. In both testate and intestate cases, the first task of an executor or administrator was settling accounts. The assets and liabilities of the estate were determined and creditors paid. The remainder of the property then went to the beneficiaries, either according to the provisions of the will or according to the law. The widow, if her husband left a will, could accept the portion he specified or request her share under intestate law. The widow of an intestate man simply received this fixed portion of the estate: a one-third life interest in a husband's real estate (half if there were no surviving children) and one-third or one-half of his personal estate with no restrictions.[5]

Pennsylvania gave preference to creditors' claims; elsewhere, debts generally could not absorb the widow's por-

tion. In Pennsylvania and most other places, personal property was first used to pay creditors; real estate was
employed only if the personal estate was inadequate for
that purpose. Whereas most colonies calculated and sheltered the widow's share from any further claims before
land was sold to pay creditors, in Pennsylvania *all* of the
testator's property was liable for debts. The widow received
her share only after every bill had been paid,[6] as William
Meredith, an estate lawyer in Philadelphia, reminded a
widowed client in 1820: "You must therefore decide
whether you will demand your legacies under the will, or
insist on your widow's share of the estate. You are aware
that whether you claim in one way or the other, your rights
must give place, to the rights of Creditors. These must be
preferred."[7]

Pennsylvania inheritance law was also unique in its
limited interpretation of the *form* of inheritance the widow
received from a particular parcel of land. In the late eighteenth and early nineteenth centuries, many states began
to permit the widow to obtain a cash equivalent for her life
interest in a third of her husband's real estate. In this way,
a widow could convert her life interest to money and thus
use or bequeath her legacy as she wished. This practice
also allowed the other heirs to sell their share of the real
estate without the encumbrance of the widow's life interest. Pennsylvania law, however, continued to maintain the
older form of the widow's life interest.[8] As late as 1832, a
law entitled "An Act relating to orphans' court" reaffirmed
this tradition. Even if real estate was converted into cash
to pay debts, the widow did not receive her share of the
surplus outright—she simply collected the interest on her
share for life.[9]

The Married Woman's Property Acts, passed in the late

1840s in many states, including Pennsylvania, changed many of the legal constraints imposed on women but did little to alter the inheritance structure for widows. The significant change was to permit a married woman to possess her own property and write a will.[10] This legislative step indirectly provided some relief for widows, who became less dependent on their husbands' legacies for their economic survival. They could maintain their own property during marriage, free from their husbands' debts, and thereby exercise more control over their economic fate if widowed.

Thus, the law in Pennsylvania did little to guarantee the rights and interests of the widow. If the law had been rigidly interpreted and enforced, Pennsylvania would have been a very inhospitable place for a woman to lose a husband. Inheritance law, however, determined the structure and parameters of the widow's share only if a man died without a will *and* his estate was settled in court. This situation was rare, as indicated by Jean Soderlund's work on Philadelphia and Chester County testation patterns. Soderlund found that among potential testators, 50 percent in Chester County and 29 percent in Philadelphia left a will.[11] Other historians, primarily in studies of New England, have made similar estimates that 20 percent to 50 percent of individuals did so.[12] Most importantly, however, Soderlund reports that only 36 percent of potential cases in Chester County, and 18 percent in Philadelphia, pursued intestate proceedings to the point of taking an inventory. These estimates suggest that a large number of widows, as many as 64 percent in Chester County and 82 percent in Philadelphia, received bequests either through a will or in some less formal manner that circumvented court action.[13] In providing for their wives, the husbands were *not* confined to the structure of a widow's share as prescribed by inheritance law.

Men who left wills had the option of being more generous to their wives than the law for intestates required. Unfortunately for the historian examining inheritance, Pennsylvania wills and inventories provide an incomplete picture of a testator's real wealth. Only the personal estate was listed in inventories, and land holdings were not regularly described in wills. There is some indication, nevertheless, that widows of testate men inherited more than the minimum share prescribed by law. A reference to the minimal dower or one-third appeared in only 38 percent of the wills examined (349 of 924). Beyond this, it is clear that in both Philadelphia and Chester County, men often gave their wives their entire estates, particularly after 1830. Together, these testation patterns imply that men were frequently more generous to their widows in their wills than required by law.

What men gave their wives if they never left a will or administrative inventory is impossible to determine definitively. Still, there are indications that although these individuals had few possessions, they gave them freely to their widows. Across the spectrum of inheritance, will-writers were probably wealthier than intestate individuals, and those who left no record of their estates were poorer on average than those who left simply an inventory.[14] This hierarchy found by scholars in probate records, particularly in New England, is partially supported by the testation patterns observed in Philadelphia and Chester County. One reason for the connection between wealth and testation patterns was that a landowner's estate had to appear in probate court for the property legally to change hands. Without a proper deed, the beneficiary could not sell the land. In Chester County, where farming was the main occupation and wealth was more evenly distributed than in the city, this legal transfer of property was crucial. In Philadelphia, with its more diversified economy, a smaller portion of people, even wealthy people, owned real property. The large number of not very prosperous households and a greater tendency to rent both homes and business properties made the probate process less important in the city.[15] Thus, in southeastern Pennsylvania those avoiding the probate process were more likely to be poorer men without real property. And these men on the lower end of the economic scale—at least among those who left wills in Philadelphia—were precisely those most likely to leave their wives a higher percentage of their estate.[16] Other historians have also found that wealthy men gave the lowest percentage of their estate to their widows and poor men gave the highest.[17] This suggests that if the men who never bothered with the probate process were generally poor, they too probably left their wives more than the legal third.

If her husband wrote a will or his estate was settled out of court, a widow had a very good chance of receiving more than her dower right. Because inheritance law actually governed the partition of a relatively small proportion of estates, we cannot assume from the start that the law had a wide impact on the construction of the widow's share in wills or less formal inheritance procedures. The rigid one-third provision was applied only when a married man died without a will and the potential beneficiaries let the legal system govern the division of the estate—and this happened only to a minority of widows in Chester County and Philadelphia.

Even though a widow depended on her husband or the law to provide her with her inheritance, she had a part to play in the male-designed and -enforced legal system. Mary Beth Norton has argued that when examining inheritance laws and probate records, the historian sees a male-constructed view of family life and its desired form after his death.[18] Although women rarely wrote wills and did not draft legislation, they should not be seen as powerless in matters of inheritance. First, some evidence suggests that women participated in the drafting of a husband's will. In addition, the occasional use of marriage agreements and trusts to protect the widow from insolvency is likely to reflect a wife's influence on inheritance patterns. There were also unofficial, even illegal, ways for a widow to augment her share of her husband's estate. Indeed, documents show women using and manipulating the "male" inheritance structure, despite the prescriptions of the legal system.

Katherine Banning Chew pursued a lengthy legal battle with her children after her husband's death in 1844, in part because she felt uniquely qualified to interpret his will.

> For Fifty five years, & five months. I was the happy wife of the best of Husbands!—and during the whole of that time I was favoured. (I believe) with His entire confidence. He considered it prudent always to have a *will* prepared to leave, in case Divine Providence should remove Him from His family—of which *Will*. He always informed me and even consulted me. I certainly never hesitated being quite satisfied with whatever He proposed.

In his original will, written in 1835, Benjamin Chew, Jr., appointed his two eldest sons and wife as executors. His

son Samuel died in 1841, necessitating a revision in the
will. "My dear Husband inquired of me, & of our eldest
son Benjamin, who we would prefer substituted in the
place of dear Samuel? We both decided, if an other is
necessary, we should prefer Mr Joseph Ingersole." In 1842
her son-in-law James Murray Mason "wrote a codicil to my
Husbands *will*" in which he named himself and two other
sons as additional executors. Katherine interpreted this
codicil as simply "a *kind compliment*" to the newly named
executors, and assumed that she and Benjamin, her eldest
surviving son, were actually to settle the estate. After
Chew's death, however, the other executors, disgruntled at
Benjamin's erratic behavior, had him and Katherine ousted
as co-executors. Although the three had a legal claim to
their offices, Katherine felt that their interpretation of the
will conflicted with her husband's intentions. "I am convinced my dear Husband could not have supposed that they
would interfere with His Eldest son, in the settlement of
the Estate, or—that they would have abused, & persecuted
His afflicted Widdow as they have done, & are yet doing."[19]
She believed that she knew his mind—and his plan for his
family—because she had discussed the will with him. She
may even have helped him write it.

In a journal written in 1799, Anne Emlen Mifflin explained her refusal to help her spouse draft a will in a way
that showed that she could, if she chose, have been involved
in the process. Warner Mifflin was a Quaker and an avid
abolitionist. Anne Emlen Mifflin, his second wife, was also
a devout Quaker and became an itinerant preacher during
her widowhood. Friends were required "to settle their affairs and make their Wills whilst in health." That Warner
became severely ill before completing his will "was the
daily, almost hourly burthen of his Soul." On his deathbed

"after repeated looks of inexpressible concern on my account, desiring me not to grieve for him," he expressed concern about his estate. Anne felt that he was "tenderly fearful that the unsettled state of affairs would be a means of adding gall to my wormwead." She considered herself partly to blame for his intestacy.

> But I could freely excuse the omission, & apply it in part perhaps to mine own doors, as he had several times in the past seasons suggested a desire that I might sympathetically aid him in forming a Will; which I regularly declined, expressing my belief that if people would enter deep to the gift of grace in their own minds—asking for aid, they might be even divinely aided in a matter of such magnitude: and in the present circumstance, as there was offspring by two Mothers, I had not a freedom to dictate, but left it entirely to the pointing of Wisdom in his own mind. Which restriction felt in myself I have had cause to be truly thankful for attending to since.[20]

Anne declined to assist Warner in constructing his will on religious grounds, and perhaps also because of her natural bias toward her own children.

One rare example of a transparent, obvious unity of opinion between a wife and her husband on the content of a will appeared in the 1841 testament of William Griffith. He stated, "I hereby sanction corroborate and confirm all the Items and particulars of a will made by my wife bearing even date with this, wherein she says as follows . . ."[21] This unusual testator then proceeded to quote his wife's will at length. Joint will-making was hardly typical, but William Griffith's suggests that a thread of female influence was present in the fabric of many men's wills.

Marriage settlements, jointure agreements, trusts, and separate estates all softened the effect of the inheritance law and reflect another form of female pressure on the rigid inheritance system. Each of these legal mechanisms gave a married woman some control over her own property and protection from her husband's creditors. They have been interpreted as simply a man's way to protect himself from insolvency (if he lost all his property, he could at least depend on his wife's sinecure),[22] or construed as dependent on the whim or generosity of the provider.[23] In either interpretation, women were simply passive recipients of increased power over their property.[24] Without attempting to replicate the work of the many legal historians who have grappled with the anomaly of separate property arrangements for married women, it is nevertheless possible to suggest alternative explanations for these provisions that attribute some more positive role to female influence.

Marriage settlements or prenuptial agreements were particularly popular among widows contemplating remarriage. Suzanne Lebsock attributes this pattern among Petersburg, Virginia, women to the wealth of widows and their concern for their children's property.[25] Marylynn Salmon argues that South Carolina widows wanted the freedom to manage their own estates after remarriage.[26] Though both explanations have validity, the most obvious reason for a widow to insist on a marriage contract would be her previous contact with the inheritance system. A widow knew first hand that even the most generous bequest from a husband could be whittled down by the demands of creditors. If her new husband neglected to write a will and she was widowed again, she might recoup only a portion of the property she had brought into the marriage. The Widow Hannah Marshall made certain that all her property was carefully listed in her marriage contract with Thomas Walker, drawn up in 1755.

> Then notwithstanding the said Marriage he the said Thomas Walker his heirs Executors Admors [Administrators] or Assigns, shall not, nor will intermeddle with, or have any right title or Interest either in law or Equity of in or to any part of the Lands Tenements Hereditements or real Estate—whereof the said Hannah Marshall is now Seized, or in or to the Rents, issue or profits thereof or any part thereof, . . . or to any Debts, Sum or Sumes of money now Due, or to become Due unto the said Hannah upon or by Vertue of any Bond, Specialty, Contract, or writing heretofore given to her, or the Interest thereof, Nor shall intermeddle with or have any right or Interest in or to the Black Walnut Desk, or pewter Dishs, and plates now in her possession.[27]

She also outlined her right to bequeath this property to whomever she wished. In addition, if Walker predeceased her, she would not be liable for his debts. Before this widow remarried, she protected herself from the harshest aspects of inheritance law.

Some marriage agreements outlined a set of mutual obligations rather than demonstrating simply female prudence or a husband's efforts to evade bill collectors. The contract between Eliza M. Crosby, widow, and Thomas Cumpston, written in 1816, provided that the resources of the couple remain separate "in all respects as if the said parties were not married," but with two specific conditions attached. Eliza, unlike a feme sole (an unmarried woman), would receive "her support and maintenance by her said intended Husband . . . during the life time of the said Thomas Cumpston." In return, Eliza would give up "all

her rights and claim to Dower or thirds in and to the Estate
and Effects of the said Thomas Cumpston which by virtue
of her said intended Marriage and by Law she may become
entitled to." This widow could keep her property intact
during marriage, and her husband freed his estate from the
encumbrance of a widow's dower right. Both parties made
concessions to achieve their specific goals.[28]

In addition to self-interest and the exchange of privileges, prenuptial agreements occasionally displayed an
equality of interests between the partners. Francis Despernay referred to his "marriage Articles" in his will of 1798.

> It is stipulated that the Goods & Estate of either of the parties
> dying before the other shall remain after his or her death the
> property of the survivor — In Consequence thereof & wishing
> to carry the said stipulation into full and complete effect, in
> case I should happen to die before my said wife, I declare by
> the present Testament that I give devise & bequeath all the
> Estate and property generally whatsoever, . . . to the said
> Louisa Frances Morel Despernay.[29]

Francis and Louisa shared equally in the proceeds of their
marital enterprise. Either would inherit the whole estate if
the partnership ended because of death. They were not
protecting their individual property from each other;
rather, they had the same wish to protect their joint property. Similarly, when Matthias Pennypacker mentioned, in
his will of 1808, the marriage contract he had made with
his wife, Mary, he referred to "our coverture."[30] A feme
covert, or a woman under coverture, was married and,
therefore, under the legal cover or protection of her husband. In becoming a wife, she left behind her right to buy
and sell property, appear in court, and write a will. A

husband also had obligations, however—specifically, to support his family. That Matthias Pennypacker felt he and his wife both entered coverture at marriage suggests that their obligations were mutual, that they were partners embarking on a joint venture.

These examples speak to the kinds of contracts women entered into and the types of relationships these represented. All of these women were careful to list their property and their privileges. They knew the legal liabilities of feme covert status and the potential harshness of the inheritance system. These contracts were signed by both husband and wife, and at least to some extent represented the concerns of both, though, distinctively, they provided the future wife with far more rights than the law allowed her. In essence, the couple collaborated and agreed on the contours of their new married life, then signed an agreement to keep them both honest and to guard against legal interference.

While women most frequently secured separate estates with male cooperation or approval in marriage contracts, some women received separate estates through the generosity of female benefactors. Suzanne Lebsock uncovered this pattern among Petersburg women, finding that the creation of separate estates by women for women became increasingly common, particularly after 1840. According to Lebsock, these benefactors were protecting their daughters and other female relatives and friends from the economic exploitation of their husbands.[31] What Lebsock fails to consider, however, is that most of the women who had the financial means and legal ability to provide another woman with independent property were widows. Their personal experience of widowhood and female vulnerability in the settlement process led them to value the protection that a separate estate provided. When a widow set up a trust for a married daughter or another woman, therefore, she may have been protecting her from a profligate husband, but more likely she was concerned with the vagaries of the legal system, which she herself had experienced.

Some Philadelphia wills demonstrate that a widow who left a separate estate to a married woman was not necessarily protecting the beneficiary from her husband.[32] Sarah P. Howard, a widow whose will was proved in Philadelphia in 1847, bequeathed property to a married daughter in trust for her use. The trustees were the executors of the estate, one of whom was this daughter's husband.[33] This widow apparently did not see her son-in-law as a potential threat to her daughter's financial well-being. Harriet Thomas's will of 1845 made David Tobias executor of her estate and gave him all her property in trust for his wife, Rachel.[34] The Widow Thomas clearly trusted him to do her bidding, and gave her friend a separate property for some reason other than buffering her against his machinations. These widows acted on the principle that a separate estate protected a married woman from a legal system that favored creditors over a dead man's family.

A widow could also use a trust to pass property down through the female line. The widow Margaret Humphreys gave her daughter, Mary Thomas, a legacy in trust, from which she received the interest while married. When her husband died, Mary would get the principal; on Mary's death, the principal would be divided among her children.[35] Ann Whittle provided her daughter with a similarly constructed legacy in her 1883 will. The daughter received the interest on $5,000; when she died, the $5,000 would go to the grandchildren.[36] A trust arrangement of this kind assured a woman beneficiary of an independent income while married and a secure maintenance if widowed; but it denied her the right to alienate or bequeath her legacy as she wished. This form of support, nevertheless, was securely protected from the legal uncertainties of feme covert status and the disadvantages of the inheritance system. It descended to the subsequent generation intact. The first concern of a widow who made such a bequest was that her property would pass through a female branch of her family without interference. To accomplish this, however, she had to be sure that a bequest was at no point left in fee simple to a woman who might remarry. If the daughter for whose line the funds were intended entered feme covert status again, the grandchildren could lose their legacies. These dynastic arrangements limited the rights of an immediate female beneficiary for the good of a later generation. The construction of such a legacy reflected an awareness of the legal realities of marriage and inheritance, and knowledge of an effective way to circumvent them.

At least in part, widows created trusts to secure a married woman's legacy within an antiquated legal structure. The law's emphasis on real property, appropriate for an agricultural community, failed to take into account the increasing importance of personal wealth in industrializing Pennsylvania. And as insolvency became more common among descendents in a more dynamic economy, the protection of personal estates from creditors took on new urgency.[37] After 1830, the number of Philadelphia widows who set up trusts to protect personal property bequeathed to married women increased significantly; previously rare, this type of bequest was utilized by 20 percent (15 of 75) of the widowed testators studied between 1830 and 1850 in Philadelphia. Chester County widows also made use of the trust after 1830, but in this still primarily rural area, the trust was useful to a smaller percentage of widows (10 percent, or 2 of 20).[38]

A woman who received the legacy of a separate estate enjoyed broadened legal and economic options and could offer certain protections to her family. Free from the claims of her husband's creditors, a wife's independent estate protected the entire family from bankruptcy during her husband's lifetime or after his death. She could use her property to help her husband, and therefore her family, out of financial difficulty. Like Deborah Norris Logan, a wife might sell her patrimony while married. In 1825, during her widowhood, she recalled the circumstances surrounding the sale of her property.

> I now remember with great Comfort, selling my last Ground Rent in Philadelphia, an annuity of 100 dollars, to relieve my beloved Husband from a perplexity of a like nature [to pay creditors],—the Relief that Dear Dr Logan expressed, more than compensated me for the sacrifice.[39]

The same flexible, constructive use of property within a loving marriage emerges from Thomas Hopkinson's will of 1751. At marriage, his wife held a patrimony in the form of land on the "Island of Antiqua." She intended to give her new husband this land "and certain Deeds of Instruements were Executed by her for that purpose." A snag developed when the new Mrs. Hopkinson was required to be "privately Examined by a Magestrate in the Leeward Islands or in Great Brittain or Ireland." Thomas discontinued his efforts,

> being assured by my said Wife that she will as soon as possible after my Decease convey and settle the said Plantation or

Tract of land in such manner that after her Decease the same
shall go to my Children to be divided among them in such
proportion as she shall think fit and having from a long
Experience of her Fidelity & discretion sufficient Reason to
depend on her promise in this matter.[40]

Separate estates, in short, enhanced the family's assets. If
the interests of the wife and husband coincided, her independent property could provide an emergency fund for the
family.

Beyond this, there is some evidence that the personal
property a married woman brought into the marriage was
often treated by the couple as her "separate estate," although before the law, without a specific agreement to
that effect, the goods were her husband's.[41] A number of
men made provisions in their wills for their spouses to
recover these items when widowed. Job Harvey made this
kind of bequest in his will of 1750/51: "I give her the Sole
Use of all those goods which she brought with her and
were hers before our Intermarriage." In the room-by-room
inventory of his estate was a page with the heading "Goods
which were his wives before their Intermarriage and By his
last Will are Bequeathed to her during her Widowhood."
Her property ranged in value from a three-shilling "Rattrap
and a Mouse trap and two brushes" to a "feather bed with
its furniture" worth £25. Included was an item that had
not been part of her dowry, "a Clothes press which she
purchased since her Marriage," worth £1.2.0. Altogether
her goods totaled £69.12.0 of the £569.4.11 estate.[42] Obviously the Harveys kept a close accounting of those things
that were "hers," even if theoretically her husband owned
everything in the house.

Among the items that Aaron Martin left to his widow

in his 1829 will were "all the furniture and her silver watch
books and other things (beds excepted) that she brought to
my house when she came." The inventory of Martin's
estate carefully delineated the different kinds of provisions
made for the widow. Under the heading "Property Bequeathed to Widow to Wit" were the livestock and other
household items worth $129.25. The "Rockin Chair" and
a few other household furnishings totaling $11.00 went to
the "widow during life." The "Widows own property,"
valued at $174.95, included three "Bed, Bedsteads, Bedding
& Curtains." The last part of the inventory referring to the
widow included cider and wine worth $9.37 ½ was desig-
nated "Liquor Bequeathed to Widow."[43] This couple clearly
saw the dowry brought into the marriage as the wife's
property even after coverture. It is also worth noting that
the widow of Aaron Martin felt that the beds should be
included among her goods, and apparently convinced the
auditors that they should be listed in her part of the
inventory.

In addition to the legally sophisticated step of arranging a
separate estate before remarrying, a woman could augment
her widow's portion through illegal methods. First, she
could manipulate her share before the settlement process
even began. The initial step in dividing a decedent's property was for the executor or administrator to take an
inventory of the estate. This inventory included all bonds,
bank notes, cash, and other personal property owned by a
man at his death. Before commencing this process, the
executor or administrator announced to the appraisers,
who would help him or her price the items, and to other
interested parties, when the inventory would be taken. To
make a probate inventory, the executor or administrator

then drew up the list of possessions, usually with witnesses present. A widow who wanted to retain certain items for herself had to act before this public process began, perhaps removing the things she wanted (or burying them in the backyard) so that they would not appear on the inventory. If she was careful, and no one missed the items, she could recover this illicit inheritance once the settlement process was over. The extent to which widows circumvented the inheritance system in such a manner is unknown; court records point only to the women whose deceptions were discovered.

The Chester County Orphans Court caught up with Abraham Bateman's widow, who tried to hide some of her husband's goods from the administrator of his estate. John Tilow, after taking his initial inventory on 1 May 1810, concluded "that there is not sufficiency of assets in the hands of the administrator of said deceased to pay the Debts due and owing from the Estate of the said Deceased." The court appointed auditors to suggest a way to divide the existing assets equitably among the creditors. The auditors made the following report to the court on 15 June 1810:

Pursant to the directions of the within order of Court We the auditors therin named have met to strike a dividend between the creditors of Abraham Bateman Deceased DO Report that in consiquence whereof a number of said Creditors came forward and produced Margaret Frederick, Catharine Tuff, James Frederick Redwalt, Jacob Keeley, and Bolsar Essick Witnesses whoes testimony proved there was property kept back or secreted by the widow of said Abrham Bateman (without the knowledge of the administrator) at the time of the appraisement which if brot. forward and sold would be sufficient to pay all the demands against the said estate.[44]

Both secrecy and knowledge of the law helped Mary Kelton enlarge her inheritance by hiding her husband's will. The 1777 last testament of James Kelton of London Grove, Chester County, provided his second wife, Mary, with all his personal property and rent from his land until their children were of age or she remarried. At the bottom of this document was Mary Kelton's signed agreement to the following statement, "Let it be remembered that my wife Mary Kelton is fully satisfied with my will by certyfying under her hand and seal that she never will desire it to be altered." When James passed away at the age of eightysix, his wife was a mere twenty-nine. No doubt unhappy with the remarriage restrictions in her husband's will, she decided to take her chances with intestate proceedings. She claimed that her husband had died without a will and that his estate should therefore be divided according to law. Mary Kelton in this manner evaded the remarriage clause of her husband's will. She took a new husband and moved to Tennessee with her inheritance apparently intact.[45]

With a blatant disregard for legal procedure, some widows took their share of an inventoried estate before it was given to them. Elizabeth Peirsol died in 1814, the year after her husband, Jeremiah. In his will, Jeremiah left his widow his whole estate and made her co-executor along with his son-in-law. She expired before collecting her $313.20 inheritance but used $109.00, a third of the estate, before her death. Her executor defined this sum as "the loss or waste of Jeremiah's property."[46] Perhaps the Widow Peirsol believed her need for the funds, due to illness, justified her behavior; or she may have felt that as the property would eventually become hers, she ought to use it. Mary Croxton displayed a similar lack of concern over the official division of her husband's estate. She and her co-administrator, Francis Smedley, inventoried Samuel Croxton's estate, worth £184.4.6. In 1757, when the estate was to be divided among the heirs and creditors, the property had diminished. Francis Smedley blamed Mary Croxton for this discrepancy.

> That the said Mary Croxton kept the said Estate altogether in her own hands for a Considerable time after the Appraisemt. was made, before any Sales thereof were made, and used and Expended Several things in the house and Elsewhere, which were Appraised, and were not to be found at the time of Sales—That the Amount of the Sales (by reason of Such delay and Waste) fell far Short of the Appraisement.[47]

In such circumstances, the worst penalty was the deduction of the stolen property's value from the lawbreaker's final inheritance. These women apparently took no more than their rightful portion and felt no compunction about taking their share early. A widow's portion of her husband's estate was determined by more than the inheritance law, and by means of a variety of devices, women clearly could soften the law's contours.

To assess the impact of the law, we must examine both how many women were affected by the legal aspects of the inheritance system and whether the women involved in fact found the system limiting.[48] To determine what the specific provisions left by a male testator meant for his widow, we must understand what being an executor signified and what women thought of that role. The executor of an estate gathered the deceased's assets together, paid the creditors, and distributed the surplus. To determine the size of a decedent's holdings, one first had to ascertain the debts owed the estate. Once all assets were identified, an inventory of the testator's uncollected debts and other personal property was made with the help of creditors, friends, or neighbors serving as appraisers. To file the inventory as required, the executor appeared in court and probably had already come before the justices to obtain official sanction to undertake the duties of the post. For those living far from the county seat, travel to court was time-consuming and might require an overnight stay. Collecting outstanding debts after the inventory was filed, another of the executor's responsibilities, could also entail considerable travel and expense, especially in the case of a complex estate. Before the property was divided, creditors were located and paid out of the personal property. If the goods and chattel of the testator were insufficient, real estate was sold. Selling land required another court appearance. After the creditors were satisfied, the surplus was finally distributed among the heirs. In a last appearance in court, the executor presented an account of the debts and credits of the estate and could then claim expenses and a 5 percent commission. In most cases, the executor's responsibilities were to be completed within a year.[49]

Contemporaries generally found the role of executor troublesome and accepted it out of personal loyalty, not for financial gain. The heirs of Jeremiah Hornketh asked the Philadelphia Orphans Court to appoint auditors to examine, among other irregularities, the executor's request for a 7.5 percent commission. The auditors' report, filed in 1830, outlined the limitations and obligations of the position of executor.

An administrator enters upon his task voluntarily—an executor takes it because such was the living wish of a dead friend—the one as an affair of legal business—the other as a sacred duty. It is true an executor may renounce—few however do this since testators select upon most occasions men of probity, those in whom confidence is to be placed and who will not abandon the charge imposed upon them. It cannot be supposed that it was ever the intention of a testator unless so expressed to impose labour without thinking of reward. He names his executor with a view to the safety of his property and a desire to serve his friend. This too is for the interest of the heirs, their inheritance comes into honest hands. Whenever their duties are faithfully discharged and the settlement of an estate has been productive of more than ordinary trouble . . . the auditors think that 5 percent would not be what they suppose commissions to mean—a compensation.

This statement emphasizes that the executor's commission was intended to compensate for a burdensome task, to reward a trusted friend for his trouble. A higher commission was judged appropriate in the cited case because of the "considerable labour" involved.[50]

In the complex and prolonged settlement of the estate of Benjamin Chew, Jr., who died in 1844, the issue of the executor's role and payment also surfaced. The executors of the Chew estate asked for a 7.5 percent commission ($12,670.09), in combination with repayment for other expenses they had accrued during the settlement process, for a total amounting to 15 percent of the entire estate. The Orphans Court found these claims reasonable, recognizing a connection between the size of the commission asked and the scope of the services rendered by the executor.

Commissions in Pennsylvania *are* allowed as a compensation, not as a profit. The office of executor is one of confidence—

not emolument. Thus the measure of allowance is the degree of trust reposed; the labor employed, and the risk run. The rate, therefore, may vary with the circumstances of every case; and while five per cent. is said to be a reasonable allowance in most cases, not more than three per cent. will be admitted when the estate is very large and easily administered; while much higher rates have been adopted, where the care and trouble were great or the circumstances required an increase.[51]

The court clearly stated that an executor was to be paid for his time, but was not to profit from his trust. A larger commission was acceptable if the executor's workload was unusually heavy. The position was a burden and a trust; the holder was to be adequately, though not lavishly, compensated.

The responsibility, time demands, and potential unpleasantness of the executor's role could make it particularly burdensome for a bereaved, and perhaps elderly or sick, woman. Benjamin Franklin Bache designated his wife, Margaret, a co-executor of his 1798 will because of his concern for her mental and physical condition.

> As any accident that might befall me, would necessarily render my dear wife unable to pay the attention which might be necessary to worldly affairs & especially should her recent disposition interfere It is my will that along with my dear wife Margaret Bache, the following persons our mutual friends be the Executors of this my last will.

Sensitive to the demands placed on a sole executor, Benjamin Franklin Bache acted out of concern for his wife's well-being, not distrust or a desire to limit her power. His generous bequest to her testifies to his intentions.

To my dear and beloved wife Margaret Bache I give and
bequeath all & Singular my Effects & Property of whatever
kind to be by her used according to her own good sense, firmly
confiding, from the tenderness & love which I have in every
shape experienced from her uniformly.[52]

This grandson of Benjamin Franklin created a will that
would shield his loved and trusted wife from undue stress
should she become his widow.

Hannah Pyle, the widow of Joseph Pyle of Chester
County, a consumptive who died within a year of her
husband's death in 1844, relied heavily on her two co-
executors to carry out the settlement of her husband's
estate. After her death, the issue of who had settled Joseph
Pyle's estate and had control of the resulting resources
came before the Orphans Court. A witness testified that
Jacob Pyle and Samuel Wickersham had divided the executorial duties between them: "Jacob Pyle paid the bills . . .
he took all the receipts[,] Jacob & Samuel came to West
Chester and attended to the business of the estate." Although she never officially renounced her executorship,
Hannah made clear to Jacob Pyle her inability to partici-
pate in the settlement process: "At the time of proving the
will she made objections to coming to West Chester, she
was not well—said she did not want anything to do with
the business, said she was not able—" Hannah did make
two trips to West Chester on estate business—when the
will was proved and when she selected a guardian for her
daughter—but told her co-executors that "she did not want
to be bothered with" the settlement process.[53] This frail
widow exercised the option provided by her husband and
depended on trusted co-executors to settle the estate.

A will does not always reveal the writer's motives, but

the provision for its execution can tell us something about a husband's affection and concern for, or mistrust of and lack of faith in, his wife. One way to approach the husband's reasoning is to examine the relationship between the widow's position as executor and the complexity of the husband's estate as indicated by his occupation.[54] Although this is a rough measure of the burden imposed on an executor, such an analysis does give some insight into when and why a widow was appointed as executor.

Testators with large and complex property holdings, labeled "upper class" in Table 2-1, rarely named their wives sole executor, preferring to make them co-executors.[55] Settling the estates of merchants, manufacturers, and other professional men in this category required much time and expense. Finding a similar pattern among wealthy Petersburg men who left wills, Suzanne Lebsock concludes that these testators believed their widows were incapable of handling a complicated estate.[56] Given the many highly competent women who surfaced in my research and the tendency among testators with large and complex estates to appoint their wives as co-executor, a desire to limit the widow's burden appears to be a better explanation. To the same point, David Narrett, in his study of colonial New York inheritance practices, concludes that merchants almost always named more than one executor simply because of the complexity of their estates; whether a man or a woman was to take on the task, the considerate testator divided it.[57] Even if a man failed to name his wife executor at all, this omission was not necessarily a negative statement about her abilities. In Walter Paxson's 1844 will, he appointed a male neighbor his sole executor. The wording of the will, however, demonstrates his abiding faith in his wife: "I bequeath to my beloved wife Hannah all the

TABLE 2-1
Class and Executorial Status of Widows in Philadelphia,
1750–1850

Class	Executorial Status (as % of Class)			Cases
	Sole Executor	Co-Executor	Not Executor	
Upper[a]	2.3	55.8	41.9	43
Middling[b]	32.3	43.0	24.7	93
Lower Sort[c]	45.5	27.3	27.3	22
Unspecified[d]	20.0	46.7	33.3	30
Total				188

Source: Philadelphia Wills, Register of Wills, Philadelphia.
Note: These occupational categories and class divisions are based on those in Susan Edith Klepp, "Philadelphia in Transition: A Demographic History of the City and Its Occupational Groups, 1720–1830" (Ph.D. dissertation, University of Pennsylvania, 1980), 329–331. The unspecified group—occupations that have an ambiguous relationship to class—and a few specific occupations not included by Klepp were taken from Gary B. Nash, The Urban Crucible: Social Change, Political Consciousness, and the Origins of the American Revolution (Cambridge: Harvard University Press, 1979), 387–391, table 1.
[a] Merchants, professionals, titled individuals, manufacturers, and miscellaneous government and private sector officials.
[b] Wood, metal, leather, textile, and other crafts, as well as white-collar workers, captains, and shopkeepers.
[c] Mariners, carters, stevedores, laborers, waiters, and porters.
[d] Yeomen, husbandmen, farmers, planters, and freeholders.

remainder of my property after the payment of my just debts having full confidence that she will appropriate it to the support of herself and my children."[58] Hannah Paxson and other widows of men with complicated estates were spared the long and tedious task of settling their husbands' estates alone.

If the role of executor was simple and straightforward, the widow most frequently got the job. Of course, testators chose executors for a variety of reasons—many of them idiosyncratic. Analysis based only on who was named executor in a will fails to consider the flexibility of informal arrangements for handling these assignments; the executors named were not always the individuals who actually settled the estate. In a sample of married male testators in Philadelphia between 1800 and 1850, 21 percent (40 of 190) of the estates were settled by a different combination of people from the individuals appointed in the wills. This reorganization of responsibility occurred typically in co-executor arrangements. A reluctant executor could resign unofficially by failing to exercise his or her right in court. If an individual never obtained letters of testamentary, whether purposely or not, he or she had no legal right to act as executor. More officially, an individual could resign or renounce his position, leaving the other executor or executors to carry out the settlement. These changes in practice resulted a third of the time (13 of 40 cases) in the widow's assuming sole executor status where she had originally been a co-executor.[59] In addition, between co-executors the division of labor was not always even. In the handling of the estate of Israel Brown, for example, the widow, Ann Brown, used her co-administrator only as a consultant. She described the work done by John Inskeep to the Philadelphia Orphans Court in 1805: "No part of the property or effects of the said Israel Brown has ever come into his hands or possession, but that they have been wholly and are at this time in my power & possession . . . & that the said John Inskeep has hitherto only assisted me with his advice & counsel."[60] A person appointed by the testator had to carry out his or her share of the executorial duties in order to influence the process of inheritance.

The legal and practical flexibility surrounding the position of executor allowed the individuals involved to determine who would actually take on the responsibility of settling an estate. The decision could be made by mutual agreement between co-executors. Enoch Lloyd of Chester County made Samuel Morris co-executor of his estate in his 1775 will without asking him. Morris renounced the executorship: "Nowing not of it until after his [Lloyd's] Death Therefore I Resign She [the widow of Lloyd] Being Willing To Take the whole mater upon her Self."[61] Similarly, a sole executor could give up her autonomy in order to limit her workload. John Heilig, in his will of 1840, left his widow, Barbara, sole executor of his estate, with the provision that "should she however find it best, and wish to have some trusty man to be Executor with her, then she has full liberty to chose whom she may think a proper person."[62] The widow could decide for herself if the settlement of her husband's affairs was too onerous.

The connection between being named executor and a widow's power or perceived abilities is indirect at best. Testators had recourse to several options in constructing their wills, and executors had some latitude in taking on the burden. A married male testator frequently tried to protect his wife from performing these responsibilities. The flexibility of the system also allowed a widow either to take on more responsibilities than prescribed by the will or to relinquish them entirely. Court records document the existence of unscrupulous executors who exploited their portion and embezzled property, but these cases are not numerous. Testators usually selected trusted friends or members of their own or their wives' family as executors. On the whole, then, a widow's role in the settlement of her husband's affairs reflected her spouse's concern for her and her personal inclinations.

Like the status of sole executor, a fee simple inheritance has been interpreted as giving the widow power and reflecting a husband's trust in her economic judgment. A fee simple bequest gave a widow full control of the inherited property. In contrast, a life estate restricted the beneficiary from selling or bequeathing the land or goods received, allowing the use of the estate only during the recipient's lifetime. A fee simple bequest was less restrictive than a life estate, but it is not so clear that this arrangement was more desirable or, in effect, allowed the widow more power over her affairs. To understand how these options were used, we need to understand how male testators and their wives viewed such provisions.

Life estate provisions were certainly the norm throughout the period studied, in both Chester County and Philadelphia. With few exceptions, testators imposed life restrictions on their wives' legacies even as the size and composition of these legacies changed.[63] A number of studies of probate records in Pennsylvania and other colonies have also found life estate provisions common among testators in the late eighteenth century.[64] Toby Lee Ditz, in her examination of Connecticut inheritance practices between 1750 and 1820, discovered that 92 percent of widows received some property for life only.[65] The prevalence of this type of legacy among married male testators in the late eighteenth and early nineteenth centuries makes the provision seem almost formulaic.

On the surface this overwhelming preference for life estate over fee simple legacies seems to signal a lack of trust in female abilities or a desire to restrict a widow's power, but testators' statements' reveal no such motives. For example, in his 1802 will John Hindman of Chester County left his widow, Hannah, "the full third of my

Estate real and personal during her natural life." He indicated no mistrust of his "dearly and well beloved wife" or lack of confidence "in her wisdom and prudence to manage everything in the best manner for the good of my family."[66] This testator obviously saw no contradiction between a life estate inheritance and his faith in her ability to handle the family finances.

For John Hindman and other testators like him, the life estate limited a widow's use of property but ensured a child's legacy if a subsequent marriage took place. In short, a man who restricted his wife's inheritance to her lifetime acted out of a desire to promote the well-being of his family. Under such an arrangement, a wife could enjoy the benefits of her legacy without jeopardizing the portion her children would receive. In contrast, a fee simple legacy, given to a woman who could remarry, provided no protection for the widow and her children against a deceitful or spendthrift second husband. If the widow chose to take on feme covert status again, her new spouse gained legal control over all her property. At least with a life estate her death allowed the legacy from her first husband to descend to their children without her second husband's interference. Many male testators in fact linked life estate provisions to a remarriage clause, stating that the widow would retain her legacy for life or until she married. The specter of a second husband, not the widow's competence or reliability, was the focus of these testators' concerns. A life estate denied the new husband the power to waste the children's inheritance.

Life estate restrictions did prevent a widow from bequeathing her legacy. If she agreed with her husband's choice of heirs, however, this prohibition had little meaning. Martha Vanderslice of Philadelphia simply restated in her will of 1761 the provisions for her son originally outlined in the will of her deceased husband, Andrew.

> I will and order that my Son Anthony Vanderslice shall have the Plantation which I now live on and possess which is Willed and Bequeathed Unto him & to his Heirs & assigns forever by the last Will & Testament of my late Husband Anthony Vanderslice deceased.[67]

That husbands and wives often discussed the type and size of legacy each child would receive seems probable, if difficult to establish unequivocally. A life estate limited the widow's ability to adjust a child's legacy, but she was not without options. The inventive widow Mary Beere outlined, in her 1804 will, a creative method of bypassing the inappropriate provisions made for her profligate son in her husband's will.

> Item as my son John Beere owes to me the Sum of eight hundred Dollars with Interest for which I have his Bond & Warrant with Judgement confessed, and as he my said son by the devise in his fathers will after my decease will inherit the Messuage and Lot of Ground wherein I now dwell and as his conduct in life makes me apprehensive that said Messuage and Lot will be seized & sold for debt therefore it is my mind and will that in case said Messuage and Lot of Ground shall be taken in execution and sold in the lifetime of him my said son or at anytime for debts his or his wife contracting their (if not paid before) my said Judgement Debt or the Account of my said Bond with all the Interest thereon accrued shall be demanded & recovered by Executors out of the proceeds of such sale—

The executors would then divide the money among her grandson and two granddaughters.[68] The inability to bequeath a property was, therefore, an encumbrance only if a widow disagreed with her husband's choice of heirs or the size of their legacies, or if changed circumstances made a bequest seem ill-conceived. Content with their husbands' wills and their children's behavior, many widows probably never thought of their limited will-making powers as a handicap.

A widow, furthermore, could always lease her property to gain some liquidity from her inheritance. To sell her home or other personal items would probably not be appealing, particularly for an elderly woman comfortable with her surroundings. Elizabeth Dowlin, widow of John Dowlin, described a life estate as advantageous in Chester County Orphans Court in 1849. The executors settling her husband's affairs offered her $1,000, either in trust for life or outright. She replied that "she wd. rather have the intrust for life than the money, because if she got the money it wd. not stay with her long, she had a large family & they were pretty hungry & wd soon get it out of her hands—"[69] This widow felt that a restricted access to her inheritance would help her budget her funds; the free use of her legacy would lead to its depletion. For some widows the option to sell their inheritance was superfluous; for others, it was undesirable.[70]

To judge by the widow's actual experience with the inheritance system in Philadelphia and Chester County in the late 1700s and early 1800s, Pennsylvania law was not as harsh on women as has been suggested. A large majority of widows apparently avoided intestate procedure altogether, receiving their portion informally or according to the provisions in a will. As a result, many women received more of their husbands' estates than the law would have provided them. Beyond this, women exercised some influence on how inheritance actually worked. A wife, through separate estate arrangements and/or collaboration with her husband on his will, could help regulate the size of her own legacy and the form of control she had over it. With legal knowledge and daring, an unscrupulous widow could go further and actually circumvent the law to augment or guarantee her portion. Usually, however, the widow's influence was subtle and, therefore, virtually undetectable. Even so, executorial assignments and fee simple bequests must be recognized as poor indicators of a widow's actual power because of the complex decision-making that governed such arrangements and the uncertain benefits that were extended to heirs through these mechanisms. In general, widows must be seen to have actively participated in the inheritance system.

Settling the affairs of a deceased husband was the important first step in establishing a widow's economic circumstances. Her transition to life without a male provider was eased if her share was ample and creditors were scarce. Yet the size of a husband's estate, once settled, was not the sole determinant of how she fared. Thereafter, the maintenance or improvement of her husband's legacy, and the benefit she derived from it, depended upon her own continuing efforts.

3

Poverty and Widowhood

The recent literature on early American society frequently equates widowhood with poverty.[1] In fact, substantial numbers of widows were poor, but not always as a consequence of their marital status. Most of these women had lived close to the poverty level all their lives. When widowed, they continued to struggle to make ends meet by combining resources from their own labor, aid from friends and family, and funds from public or private charities. As is true of other people living on the edge, a change in their health or a downturn in the economy could mean disaster. With careful management and some luck, however, the poor widow could maintain a meager existence outside the almshouse. This chapter examines how widows of very limited resources supported themselves or became public charges, and what life at this margin meant for widowed women.

For most poor women, widowhood simply exacerbated the poverty they had known while married. Most paupered widows had been wives of men who worked in low-paying jobs, and many had themselves labored for wages during marriage in order to supplement their family's income.

They frequently moved from place to place in search of employment. The few poor widows who had come from better circumstances made sure that the Guardians of the Poor knew that they, unlike other paupers, deserved respect and sometimes special treatment.

After 1822, the Philadelphia almshouse kept a detailed account of all legal residents who entered the institution.[2] Occasionally the information given by widowed inmates included the occupation of their deceased husbands. Among the women who offered such information between 1822 and 1844, 49 percent (17 out of 35) named jobs that identify their husbands as having a meager income; 34 percent (12) were married to men of slightly higher economic status; while only 17 percent (6) had a spouse who might be called middle-class. None had a husband who could be classified as well off.[3] Catharine Buckley, a forty-three-year-old widow, described to the Overseers her material circumstances while her husband was still alive:

> That they built a shanty & lived in it about three months when it was thrown down by the blasting of a Rock by which accident she lost one of her children, & shortly after buried the other, they then occupied another shanty & lived in it nearly *two years*.[4]

For this woman, life *before* the loss of her husband involved desperate poverty and inadequate, dangerous housing. Widowhood and residence in the almshouse made little change in her economic circumstances.

The substantial number of women who worked during their married lives to bolster their family's scant income had held jobs as diverse as paper mill worker, coal miner, and, most commonly, domestic servant.[5] In a statement given to the Overseers in the 1830s, Maria Pucé Simmons described how she and her husband, William, supported themselves and their two children.

> Said Simmons was a labouring man, followed Digging wells, driving cart or jobbing about the city & did not live with her as a Husband, had no fixt place of residence—That she was hired out to do House work, living as a domestic in other peoples houses &c.[6]

These women, when widowed, not surprisingly continued to labor for wages to support themselves and their children.

A marginal economic status entailed frequent relocation. Mary Ann Hasty, widowed for six months at the age of twenty-eight, described her whereabouts for the last five years when she entered the Philadelphia almshouse in 1828.

> She worked 6 months for Wm. Adams who lived on an adjacent farm, she next lived with Joshua Hasty 5 months same neighborhood, next lived with her aunt, Nancy Taylor, living 2 miles from her Uncle, for 2 months, next came to this City & lived with James Cletchen, Tavernkeeper, Spruce Street near the Delaware, for 3 months, next lived with George Lee Sadler in Spruce Street for 3 months, next went to housekeeping in Water Street, above Spruce Street in a Cellar, for 9 months, next in Fitzwater street for a year, paid 50 cents a Week, next in a house in Spruce Street belonging to George Lee for 5 months, broke up house keeping, & has been *knocking about.*[7]

Most women who had experienced this kind of nomadic existence during marriage continued to do so after its dissolution.

The occasional exception to such personal histories of ongoing poverty is the widowed almshouse resident who lays claim to a previously higher status. Mary Craig, who entered the Philadelphia almshouse in 1827 at the age of seventy-two, made sure that her short biography included the information that she "owned 600 Acres of Land at one time."[8] Similarly, Rebecca Moore, described as "a superannuated, infirm old woman," proudly identified herself at her admission into the same institution in 1792 as "once in possession of a Considerable property & once the wife of Dobbins the Butcher."[9] These women wanted to be distinguished from the less genteel members of the poorhouse community. Mary Marriot, admitted in 1757 with her daughter, asked for special privileges based on her former economic status.

> That altho' She is thankful that herself & Daughter are so well provided for, with all the necessarys of Life, & in so plentiful a manner, Yet as they were both brought up in a delicate way, begs leave to assure us, that the Provisions of the Almshouse are generally too gross for their nice Stomachs, & especially at Breakfast, & Supper Times; neither is there care taken to provide anything pretty for them, to Sup, in the Afternoons; they therefore beg the favour of us to desire you to take this Important affair into your most serious Consideration & if you find the case fairly Represented, You may allow them Tea, Coffee, Chocolate or any thing else that you verily belief will be more agreeable to their palates.[10]

The sarcastic tone of this letter makes it clear that the Overseers found such pretensions out of place and comical. Most widowed inmates were used to life without chocolate and afternoon tea.

Just as poverty was not new to most poor widows, coping with an economically precarious existence was a familiar struggle. Wage work staved off the need for charity, or supplemented what alms could be obtained.[11] Historians have recognized that widows were a significant portion of the female work force, citing numerous examples, particularly in city directories and the census, of widowed boardinghouse owners, shopkeepers, and seamstresses.[12] Unfortunately, such studies fail to take into account the full range, perhaps even the most common types, of female occupations. Some insight into this marginal world of female employment is provided by the Register of Relief Recipients, kept by the Guardians of the Poor in Philadelphia between 1828 and 1832.[13] The Overseers asked applicants what their occupation was (Table 3-1). Women like Mary Armstrong, who "sells cakes," Grace Babbs, who "sews carpet rags," Mary Bunting, who "sews a little," Margaret Fisselbaugh, who "Rocks cradle," and Priscilla Bright, who "works a little," were not the kind of individuals found in the directories or census lists. These widows lived from day to day and found work when they could. Among widows requesting "outdoor relief"—aid administered outside the almshouse—63 percent worked at some sort of paid job.

The low pay and fluctuating demand for marginal occupations often required a widow to take on several tasks to attain an adequate income. Lavinia Cummells, a forty-year-old woman who entered the Philadelphia almshouse in the 1830s, claimed that she "maintained herself by washing &c." Her widowed mother, who lived in Norristown, "keeps House, cooks & takes in washing."[14] Harriet Ward, a twenty-three-year-old widow with one child, reported to the Overseers on her admission to the almshouse

TABLE 3-1
**Occupations of Widows on Outdoor Relief in Philadelphia,
1828–1832**

Occupation	Number	Percent
Sewing	93	28.6
Seamstress	2	0.6
Tayloress	2	0.6
Sewing and washing	1	0.3
Spooling	25	7.7
Knitting	3	0.9
Spinning	1	0.3
Selling cakes	11	3.4
Selling in market	5	1.5
Sewing, cutting, or selling carpet rags	2	0.6
Shopkeeping	1	0.3
Selling earthenware in market	1	0.3
Huckstering	1	0.3
Rocking cradle	2	0.6
Keeping a child	2	0.6
Minding a child	1	0.3
Nursing a child	1	0.3
Washing	28	8.6
Doing housework	6	1.8
Shoebinding	4	1.2
Nursing	4	1.2
Teaching	1	0.3
Sugarmaking	1	0.3
Assisting daughter	1	0.3
Unspecified	5	1.5
Unknown	11	3.4
None	110	33.8
Total	325	

Source: Register of Relief Recipients, 1828–1832, vol. 2, Guardians of the Poor, Philadelphia City Archives, Philadelphia.
Note: See n. 13 to Chapter 3 for information on sample.

that she had "supported herself by going out to days work,—taking in washing & Ironing, &c."[15] With a combination of odd jobs, a woman could often avoid reliance on the benevolence of others, or at least escape the rigors of the almshouse.

Poor widows were acutely aware of the connection between their own labor and their ability to avoid the almshouse. After forty years of widowhood, Elizabeth Ford, at age seventy-three, could no longer support herself. She entered the poorhouse in 1802. Judging from the Overseer's description of this "aged, infirm woman," she had no choice: "Elizabeth has struggled hard for a livelihood, but age and infirmity now renders her incapable of providing for herself a support, & being poor & no *friends to help* her, she is come in."[16] Rosannah Davis, who came into the almshouse for the second time on 13 March 1800, struggled despite ill health to escape the confinement of institutional life through employment.

> She was here in July 1799 with her Son, and had a bad sore leg then; they were only dischd the 28th last. January. Her leg at that time being so that she thought herself able to work out at Service for a living, but it getting bad again, in the interim of her service as house Maid with John Mease No 5 Norris's Alley, he procur'd an Order of Admission for her from W. John Wagner and was brought here in a Harness'd Chair.[17]

Without the income she had obtained through domestic service, the Widow Davis could not maintain herself outside the almshouse. Having some kind of work, however mixed or marginal, was the first line of defense in the fight against destitution.

Even if a widow held onto a job, she still had to grapple

with the loss of her husband's income. Regardless of the kind, or number, of occupations she engaged in, her low wages—usually one-half to one-third those of male wage earners—could not make up for this deficit.[18] To augment her wages or reduce expenses, the widow had several options.

Sharing a residence was one economy measure, but living as a dependent in the home of a child or other relative was not so prevalent as one might believe.[19] The federal census is not helpful in determining the relationship of household members to the head of the household before 1850, but a census of pensioners taken in 1841 contradicts the conventional view of the housing patterns among poor widows.[20] In Chester County the proportion of widows among pensioners was too small (2 out of 26) to allow any generalizations. In Philadelphia, 40 of 84 pensioners (47 percent) were widows, their mean age being seventy-seven years. Among these women, the housing arrangements of 10 percent were unknown, 20 percent resided in the home of someone with the same last name, 30 percent headed their own household, and 40 percent lived in the home of someone with a different last name. Although those who lived with a married daughter would be included in the latter category, the fact that widows Edith Nunemaker and Mary Levering both resided in the home of Joseph H. Hoffman suggests that some of these women were living in boardinghouses. Many widowed pensioners apparently lived outside the family circle.

Poor widows, to help defray the cost of housing or perhaps to ease their loneliness, frequently turned to other single women in similar circumstances as living companions. Such an arrangement was described in the Examination of Hannah Booth on her entry into the Philadelphia almshouse. She had "hired a room (in connection with Ellen Jones) in Mary Street, from Mr. Streatcher occupied it jointly for 12 months, (between them) paying 75 cents per week rent for the same."[21] That women commonly shared quarters to minimize expenses can be inferred from outdoor relief lists that included the addresses of widowed paupers. The 1814–1815 list, in particular, shows a clustering of widows on certain streets and alleyways. Although street numbers appear only sporadically, a few women obviously lived in a boardinghouse of some kind. Ann Marlow gave her address as "Arch St. at Mrs. Bakers," Catherine Rhine resided "At Mr. Wescotts Arch above 9th," and Lucy Barry lived "Between Library & Walnut at Mr. Cannan's." A few of the paupers boarded in the same establishment or at least shared the same home. Mary Keemley and Catharine Weyman both lived at "No. 28 Sugar Alley."[22] Hannah Bigard and Lydia Branton, on the 1828–1832 outdoor relief list, shared a residence at "163 St. Johns."[23] Poor widows lived on the same streets and alleys, and at times in the same houses. These arrangements made life outside the almshouse possible for some women. Nevertheless, many had to turn to various forms of charity.

Probably the most common form of charity available, but the hardest to identify, was that received from friends or generous strangers.[24] A gift to pay funeral expenses or provide for hungry children could help a widow make the transition to life alone. Friends might provide a widow with a place to live, free from the need to rely on family or public accommodations. Beyond that, more distant acquaintances or even strangers sometimes took an interest in a particular widow's plight; a former employee or respectable older woman might receive assistance from a concerned individual. Some widows went from door to door in search of alms. For people with the resources to help, the widow was an appropriate object of charity.

Susanna Seyfried recounted to the Philadelphia Orphans Court in 1801 the assistance she received from her friends. After her husband "died of the Yellow Fever in the Year 1798," her economic circumstances went from bad to worse.

> That all the little Articles they possessed of Personal Property was taken to pay the Rent that she had only her Bed left that since that time she hath with great difficulty procured subsistence for herself and the Infant Child She has living by the said Jacob Seyfried.

Friends came to her aid during this crisis: "The Funeral and Expenses attendant she paid out of Monies received from her Friends."[25] Similarly, Margaret Fullerton's application for a pension in 1791 outlined the crucial role her friends had played in her financial survival since her husband's death in 1776: "Without the assistance she received from some of her friends she could not have supported herself & four helpless Children."[26] Friendship meant financial survival for these widows.

A lack of friends forced others into the almshouse: One of the reasons women listed for entering the Philadelphia poorhouse was "no friends." The young widow Elizabeth Davis limped into the city from Princeton with a bad case of pleurisy. She arrived in Philadelphia on 30 April 1802 and approached the almshouse the next day, "having neither money or friends."[27] Conversely, Susannah Good left the almshouse, with the help of her friends, after four and a half years there.

Discharged. Susannah Good Widow of Jacob Good, who died on Friday last, these old couple have been in the house upward of four years & a half, during which time they conducted themselves, decently, orderly, and in a becoming manner, she was (with the approbation of the visiting Committee) taken out by her friends, who will provide and take care of her.[28]

The contrasting experiences of Elizabeth Davis and Susannah Good demonstrate that friends could provide a buffer between the pauper and the almshouse.

Soliciting charity from strangers was another informal method of supplementing a meager income. The wealthy Quaker widow Sarah Pemberton Rhoads listed the amounts she gave to beggars in her daybooks, kept from 1796 to 1798 and again fron 1801 to 1803. These people visited her at least once a month, and sometimes once a week. She gave them amounts ranging from eleven pence to five dollars. She was most generous, however, to her friends and to widows. In fact, widowed beggars were often listed by name in her ledger. "Gave Mary Donald a poor Widow one dollar." Most of the people the Widow Rhoads aided had less personal entries, such as "a poor Woman," "a Beggar," "a poor lad."[29] Widows could perhaps expect more generosity from a wealthy woman who had also felt the pain of loss.

Wealthy men also provided widows with support. John Elliot Cresson found Catharine Beale wandering the streets of Philadelphia and felt moved to give her assistance. This widow was "very ancient and infirm, being nearly blind and scarcely able to walk; she came in a Carriage accompanied by Mr. John Elliot Cresson, who seems to have paid very great attention to her, on account of being a pious deserving Woman," recorded the Guardians of the Poor.[30]

Even the less-than-pious widow was a proper object of charity if she had once been part of the almsgiver's household. After the death of her husband, Rees, during the yellow fever epidemic of 1798, Margery Olliver no longer "behaved herself in an Orderly manner," but took on "a propensity for drunkeness." She was a servant in the home of Richard Bache for many years and then took up residence in the home of Peter Browne, Esq. When her decline into intemperance began, Bache's son-in-law, John Harwood, took in her only child, Eliza. Peter Browne wrestled with the burden this former servant represented.

> This poor woman has lived in the family of Peter Browne Esq. who did all in their power to restrain her from intemperate drinking, but to no purpose; she has such a propensity for drunkeness that they were obliged to part with her, and with their assistance she got to housekeeping; a short time since and from which to the present time she has been in a state of intoxication, that she is now deprived of her reason, and for fear she wou'd commit some act of violence on her self, Abm Garrigues and Peter Browne Esqr. has interfered and *sent her into* this house.[31]

A sense of civic duty and perhaps the specter of their own death and their wives' future, moved these men to charity.

Nonfamilial, informal aid appears only sporadically in the extant record. Helping a friend in need, giving alms to a beggar, or caring for a elderly or troubled pauper was, however, probably more common than the sparse citations suggest. When historians examine the sources of support for the poor in the late eighteenth and early nineteenth centuries, they concentrate on private and public *institutions* dispensing alms and wonder how the poor survived.[32]

Part of the answer to this question, for widows, besides the marginal occupations that boosted their income and the complex housing arrangements that reduced their spending, was apparently the incidental and sometimes systematic kindness of friends and strangers.

Private organizations, like private individuals, extended aid to poor widows, but the type of woman they helped was subtly different. A favorite object of charity among private organizations was the relatively unusual widow of means who found herself in reduced circumstances.[33] Most of the records that survive from these institutions give a thorough chronicle of the kindly matrons who devoted their time to the organization, but little information about the women they helped. One of the rare glimpses of the women who entered such institutions appears in the records of the Indigent Widows' and Single Women's Society. During an 1852 drive for funds to refurbish its Asylum, founded in 1817, the society's goals and accomplishments were briefly described in the resolution to solicit contributions.

> The Society has for its only object to furnish a decent home for aged and destitute females of meritorious character. It is conducted under the direction of a board of ladies, with exact regard to economy; its expenditures averaging somewhat less than $60 a year, or $1 15 a week for each person under its charge. It has no sectarian character. Since the commencement of its operations, it has received 284 inmates into the asylum, of whom 62 remain there now, their ages varying from 64 to 99 years.[34]

This organization catered to a select group of elderly women who were members of the "worthy" poor. An inmate had to pay a thirty-dollar admission charge and provide appropriate room furnishings and attire.[35] Sarah Day received permission to enter the Asylum in 1853 after approval by the Board of Managers. She could come to her new home after "paying her entrance fee to the Treasurer Mrs. Jones Race St. below 7th St. and giving the Matron notice two days before she is ready to go in."[36] Beyond the entrance fee, some widows also paid a weekly sum. Hannah Tumey in 1835 gave the Managers $1.50 a week, or $78.00 year from the annual pension of $80.00 she received from the government.[37]

The Widows' Asylum, as it was sometimes called, was comfortable and homey. The belongings of Fanny Collins at her death in 1831 suggest the environment in which she lived. Normally the institution kept such items in payment for expenses, but because the Widow Collins was a recent arrival, it was decided to keep only her money. The Manager's list of property to be sent to her sister specified:

> A Bed Bolster & pillow, a Bedstead, a Comfortable, a patch work spread, one Blanket, one pair Sheets, one pair pillow Cases, one hair Trunk a Bonnet and B. box, one basket, a pretty good Cloak, a fur tippet, a good Callico wrapper, Eleven Dresses & new Callico for another, 16 Muslin Capes, 3 good Shawls (Morning) one Merino, one cape, and one Muslin ditto, 12 bobbnet caps, 10 petticoats of different kinds, 2 pair Woolen stockings in ditto cotton 2 of which are new, 11 Shemeses, 4 night gowns, 5 aprons, 3 pair shoes, one of socks, 3 reticules 2 pair pockets, Silver Spectacles ditto thimble, & six dollars, Eighty nine cents in Silver found in her purse, & several small boxes containing sewing utensils, etc.[38]

The widow's own furniture and clothing tempered the experience of institutional life with their comfort and familiarity.

Private institutions such as the Indigent Widows' and Single Women's Society catered to an elite group of poor women with the proper credentials. Wealthy women solicited funds from wealthy men for formerly comfortable, if not wealthy, widows. Private charitable organizations did little to ameliorate the condition of the more numerous population of chronically impoverished widows.

Pension funds based on a husband's former occupation, ethnic background, race, or military service ensured that some other respectable middling or working-class widows avoided poverty.[39] The size of a widow's annuity depended on what her husband had put into a fund, or his rank in the military. The Presbyterian Ministers' Fund, for example, provided seven pounds in return for every two pounds invested.[40] A minister's wife, therefore, received a pension based on the financial commitment her husband had made to the organization. In a parallel fashion, state and federal pensions varied with the rank of the deceased veteran. The normal annuity was based on a half- or quarter-pay system that gave high-ranking officers and their widows considerably more than former privates and their surviving spouses.[41]

These pension funds, like private charitable institutions, serviced only a fraction of the total population of widowed paupers. Although eligible, many women of comfortable means never felt the need to rely on such charity. As Susannah Jacquet informed the Philadelphia Orphans Court in 1791, after the death of her second husband, "Your petitioner is constrained to mention that she is now reduced almost to poverty, otherwise she did not intend to apply for the half pay to which she is by law intitled as the widow of the aforesaid Joseph Jacquet."[42] Perhaps the stigma attached to receiving alms in any form prevented

widows unfamiliar with poverty from asking for help unless their circumstances became desperate. The small
number of "worthy" widows who relied on private charity,
some of them clearly not calling upon other sources that
were open to them, suggests that most widows from middling circumstances successfully escaped this humiliation.

For the poor woman who found herself a poor widow,
outdoor relief supplemented her own efforts to maintain
her meager lifestyle. With a marginally adequate occupation, frugal living arrangements, help from friends or charitable strangers, and good luck, she could support herself
with the added assistance of a weekly allowance or occasional pile of wood from the Guardians of the Poor.[43]

Chester County's system of outdoor relief paralleled
Philadelphia's, with variations that reflected the commu-
nal values of this rural county. A committee visiting the
poorhouse in 1842 commented on the kind of aid given to
paupers outside the institution.

> In our county those of the Poor who have relatives or friends
> that are able and willing to take charge of them at a moderate
> compensation, receive such pecuniary aid from the county,
> but where such is not the case they become the inmates of
> the county house.[44]

In Chester County, unlike Philadelphia during this period,
the Guardians of the Poor preferred to dispense home-
based care, with a weekly allowance given to the widow's
caretaker.

Women identified as widows in the Chester County
Outdoor Allowance Books between 1801 and 1843 received
weekly sums—or, more precisely, their caretakers received
funds for them.[45] Allowances ranged from a low of twenty-

five cents a week to a high of seventy-five cents, depending in part on the number of children the widow had to support. The more dependents a widow had, the more money she received. Rebecca Barnard received seventy-five cents a week in 1824 "to aid her in keeping her four children vizt. Margaret Jane Barnard William Smith Barnard 5 and John Barnard 2 yr..6 mos and Joseph Barnard 8 months."[46] Aid declined if the children moved away from home. Betty Chalfant, the mother of four children, had her allowance decreased on 25 March 1828 to "50 Cents weekly" because she was "very old." By 23 October 1838 she received only thirty-seven and a half cents per week.[47] Her allowance was cut as her children left home. These changing allowances simply reflected the cost of boarding the widow alone or along with her family.

The allowance system gave the caretaker limited responsibility and the widow freedom of choice. The individual who agreed to board a widowed pauper absorbed her meager weekly income. Family or friends alike received compensation when they took on the role of caretaker. The fifty cents a week Elizabeth Way collected from the Guardians went to "her Grand Son" until Sarah Hutchinson took over the responsibility of caring for her in 1818.[48] To some extent the county paid individuals to take in a pauper they might otherwise have had to care for without remuneration, so that the allowances permitted poor relations or friends to help a destitute widow without jeopardizing their own economic well-being. At the same time, regularization of this loosely structured, community-based welfare system provided extra protection for the alms recipient. A widowed pauper was no longer subject to the charitable inclinations of family and friends. She paid her own way and therefore found it easier to procure a place of

residence; if mistreated, she could move, with her allowance, to a better situation. Similarly, if a poor widow's
maintenance became burdensome, a caretaker could free
himself or herself from the responsibility for her care
without endangering her welfare.

In fact, a widowed outdoor relief recipient might move
frequently. Between 1819 and 1824, Mary Russel lived with
five different individuals for various lengths of time. She
first resided with William Brinton for almost a year. She
then moved in with Albin Harvey for ten months. After
only a month at Thomas Burnet's home (he, interestingly,
refused to be paid for his kindness), the Widow Russel
boarded with John Baldwin for fourteen weeks. After a five-
month stay with Jonathan Langley, she then returned to
Albin Harvey's dwelling for approximately two more years.
Her final place of residence was the almshouse, where she
died in 1824.[49]

In Chester County, outdoor relief provided a place for
the pauper within the community system. With a small
weekly allowance, widows and other poor county residents
mostly found shelter among friends and family. The
Guardians wanted the poor to live among people who knew
them and cared about them, yet without imposing unnecessary obligations or economic strain. In this more closely-
knit rural community, concern for less fortunate family
members and acquaintances was consistent with a com-
munally structured almsgiving system.

In Philadelphia, the problem of poverty defied any management system based on face-to-face intimacy. John K.
Alexander has estimated that 15 percent of Philadelphians
between 1760 and 1800 were poor.[50] Gary Nash has made a
smaller estimate for the Revolutionary period, concluding
that 71 out of every 1,000 city-dwellers struggled with

poverty.[51] The absolute number of poor people in Philadelphia, together with the flow of immigrants who lacked family or friends in the city, precluded an outdoor relief system based on Chester County's home-care design. The Philadelphia Guardians simply gave the charity recipient an allowance or such necessities as food, clothing, or wood, to use as he or she saw fit. This system provided the pauper with some autonomy but less security.

The recipients of outdoor relief in the city were overwhelmingly female, a good proportion being widowed. Priscilla Clement has estimated that in 1814 and 1815, 86 percent of outdoor relief paupers were women.[52] About 38 percent of those women were widows.[53] Susan Grigg, in her study of the dependent poor of Newburyport, Massachusetts, in the beginning of the nineteenth century, found that four-fifths of women collecting outdoor relief were widows.[54]

The preponderance of widows among recipients of this form of charity was in part a function of their usual classification as members of the "worthy" poor. Within the almshouse authority structure of Managers (who ran the administrative end of the operation) and Overseers (who worked more directly with the poor), however, a debate surfaced in the late eighteenth century over the purpose of outdoor relief and its effect on the individual recipient. The Managers felt that outdoor pensions were expensive and encouraged idleness among the poor, and that these paupers should, therefore, be aided within the almshouse. The Overseers saw the outdoor relief paupers as a better breed than the almshouse paupers and argued that the former should receive funds without being forced to mix with the poorhouse rabble. In 1769 the Managers succeeded in temporarily outlawing outdoor relief, or at least limiting it to aid in kind. A similar discussion brought the system to a halt again in 1828.[55] The two populations did in fact differ in both gender and marital status.

Widows received outdoor aid not only because they were seen as worthy, but also because they requested this form of alms. In their struggle to maintain themselves, outdoor relief often made the difference between success and failure. Ann Eliza Weston, a thirty-two-year-old pauper with three children, described the role outdoor relief played in her efforts to support herself and her offspring.

> [She] rented a House of the widow of the aforesaid squire Jones, situated near Mayland's Mill, in which herself & her two Children, (one of them about "three" & the other about four years of age) lived for the space of *Eighteen months* at the rate of $30 per annum, & paid the Rent out of her *"own earnings*—working at Mayland's Mill—Deponent further saith that she applied to the overseers of *Kingsessing* Township, while thus living in the Borough of West—Philadelphia (having at that time no legal settlement therein) for support to the above mentioned children, & that the said overseers, allowed the "one dollar per week" for that purpose, & also sent her some wood in the winter season to keep them warm, while she was at work at the Mill above mentioned.[56]

Most of the widows on outdoor relief in Philadelphia, like the Widow Weston, used their allowance to supplement their wages or other sources of income. This weekly sum was part of a economic package of basic subsistence.

Priscilla Clement has argued that the average amount of outdoor assistance given to paupers in Philadelphia was insufficient for their support. Using the lowest wage rates of the period as a measure (for women, $1.25 per week as a domestic servant; for men, $1.00 a day as a common laborer), Clement concluded that the fifty to seventy-five cents a week normally given to outdoor relief recipients was woefully inadequate.[57] The figures on widowed paupers gleaned from the 1814–1815 and 1828–1832 Register of Relief Recipients compare closely with Clement's estimates—sixty cents a week and fifty cents a week respectively. An outdoor relief allowance, however, was not the widow's *only* source of income. Most of these women also worked, or received aid from friends, family, or even other charitable organizations. The aged Hannah Campbell, in addition to her thirty-seven and a half cents a week from the Guardians, received the same amount from her church, also on a weekly basis.[58] Beyond this, as in the case of Ann Eliza Weston, poor widows received occasional aid in kind in conjunction with a cash allowance. In effect, outdoor relief provided a supplemental and somewhat steady source of income for the woman of little means who tried to make ends meet through some creative combination of work, charity, and reduced spending.

The typical widowed recipients of outdoor relief in Philadelphia between 1828 and 1832 lived in the Northern Liberties, were born in the region, were elderly, and needed aid because of illness. Compared with the widows confined in the almshouse in Philadelphia, these women represent an appreciably older, more stable population. They were the ones fortunate enough to maintain some semblance of independence outside an institutional setting.

Widows who appeared on the outdoor relief list came overwhelmingly from the northern part of Philadelphia County (Table 3-2). Almost half of the widows aided (45.2 percent) came from the Northern Liberties, Penn Town-

TABLE 3-2
District of Residence for Widows on Outdoor Relief in Philadelphia, 1828–1832

District	Number	Percent	District Population as Percent of City Total[a]	
Northern (City)	66	20.3	37.2	54.2
Southern (City)	55	16.9		
Southwark	57	17.5	___	14.0
Northern Liberties/Penn Township	112	34.5		
Penn Township/Kensington, Unincorporated Northern Liberties	6	1.8	45.2	31.8
Penn Township	18	5.5		
Kensington and Unincorporated Northern Liberties	11	3.4		
Total	325			

Source: Register of Relief Recipients, 1828–1832, vol. 2, Guardians of the Poor, Philadelphia City Archives, Philadelphia.
Note: See n. 13 to Chapter 3 for information on sample.
[a] Based on 1830 census. The census figures were taken from John Daly and Allen Weinberg, *Genealogy of Philadelphia County Subdivisions* (Philadelphia: City of Philadelphia, Department of Records, 1975), 93.

ship, or Kensington. Also disproportionately represented were widowed residents of Southwark (17.5 percent). The 37.2 percent of widows who came from the city were in fact proportionally the smallest group when the population of the city relative to other parts of the county is taken into account. These paupers lived on the poorer outskirts of the city. About 50 percent of the widowed women receiving outdoor alms in Philadelphia had been born in

Pennsylvania, and 30 percent in Philadelphia County itself (Table 3-3). Most widowed recipients of outdoor charity made their homes in Philadelphia and remained in the city after losing their husbands.

Most of these long-time Philadelphia residents were elderly (Table 3-4). No less than 60.3 percent of the widows receiving outdoor relief were between sixty and seventy-nine years old. Their age alone did not prevent them from maintaining themselves outside the almshouse. Without infirmity, age did not necessarily lead to dependence. In fact, if a widow had grown old in the city, her network of family and friends allowed her more economic options than a young woman who had recently arrived.

Indeed, among widowed paupers, the reason most often given for needing a weekly allowance was sickness, not the infirmities of old age (Table 3-5). Illness prevented the widow from working regularly. Since two-thirds of these women listed some occupation (Table 3-1), bad health meant underemployment. These women were able to work on occasion, but needed a supplemental income. Susan Carbon, at seventy-eight, asked for outdoor relief because of her "Inability to follow her business as Huckster."[59] Elizabeth Brotherton listed sewing as her occupation at the age of seventy-three. Ill health and the marginal nature of her job (phrased as "low wages & unable to work much") caused her to apply for outdoor relief.[60]

There is some evidence to suggest that, when able to support themselves, widows turned down an outdoor allowance. Most widows taken off the list of charity recipients between 1828 and 1832 (Table 3-6) had moved out of the area or died (62.4 percent). A few, however, actually asked to be struck from the rolls. Ann Clark, who had solicited the Guardians for aid in January 1829 because of

TABLE 3-3
Place of Birth for Widows on Outdoor Relief in Philadelphia,
1828–1832

Birthplace	Number	Percent
PENNSYLVANIA (46.7%)		
Philadelphia	96	29.5
Surrounding Counties	14	4.3
Other Pennsylvania	42	12.9
SURROUNDING STATES (16.6%)		
New Jersey	38	11.7
New York	3	0.9
Delaware	8	2.5
Maryland	5	1.5
EUROPE (34.1%)		
Ireland	61	18.8
England	3	0.9
Scotland	1	0.3
Wales	2	0.6
Germany	43	13.2
Switzerland	1	0.3
OTHER (2.4%)		
Canada	3	0.9
New Providence	1	0.3
At sea	1	0.3
UNKNOWN	3	0.9
Total	325	

Source: Register of Relief Recipients, 1828–1832, vol. 2, Guardians of the Poor, Philadelphia City Archives, Philadelphia.
Note: See n. 13 to Chapter 3 for information on sample.

a "Sprained Arm," by April of the same year had told them she "can do without."[61] Occasionally a widow's condition foiled her attempt to free herself from the necessity of

TABLE 3-4
Age of Widows on Outdoor Relief in Philadelphia, 1828–1832

Age	Number	Percent
14	1	0.3
20–29	4	1.2
30–39	24	7.6
40–49	20	6.2
50–59	28	8.6
60–69	101	31.1
70–79	95	29.2
80–89	40	12.3
90–99	6	1.8
100–111	5	1.5
Unknown	1	0.3
Total	325	

Source: Register of Relief Recipients, 1828–1832, vol. 2, Guardians of the Poor, Philadelphia City Archives, Philadelphia.
Note: See n. 13 to Chapter 3 for information on sample.

public relief. Mary Curry, afflicted with Rheumatism," had to request relief again after being "struck off at her request" because her condition rendered her unable to support herself by needlework.[62]

The widow on outdoor relief in Philadelphia used her weekly allowance to supplement her efforts to support herself through employment and aid from networks of family and friends. Most often, as an elderly, long-term resident of the city, she used her knowledge of the community and its resources to remain free of the almshouse if she could.

As with outdoor relief, the Chester County and Philadelphia almshouses supported the needy in a manner that was

TABLE 3-5
Reasons for Poverty for Widows on Outdoor Relief in
Philadelphia, 1828–1832

Reason[a]	Number	Percent
Sickness	269	66.1
Rheumatism	13	3.2
Injury	4	1.0
Pregnancy	1	0.3
Mental illness	1	0.2
Young children	12	2.9
Children who cannot help	12	2.9
Sick children	8	2.0
Dependency on children	2	0.5
Old age	46	11.3
Poverty	16	3.9
Inability to work	10	2.5
Loss of husband	6	1.5
Low pay	2	0.5
No friends	2	0.5
Unknown	3	0.7
Total	407	

Source: Register of Relief Recipients, 1828–1832, vol. 2, Guardians of the Poor, Philadelphia City Archives, Philadelphia.
Note: See n. 13 to Chapter 3 for information on sample.
[a] Of the 325 individual cases aided, some widows had more than one reason for poverty. Each reason was counted separately.

consistent with the nature and size of each community. The Chester County poorhouse, situated on a farm in West Bradford, opened its doors in October 1800. Until 1855, all the dependent poor of this rural community (except for some sick people who were put in the poor hospital after 1811) lived in a single 40 by 100 foot brick building. In the first year, 94 paupers entered it. By the year 1823, there were 301.[63]

TABLE 3-6
Reasons for Widows' Removal from Outdoor Relief List in Philadelphia, 1828–1832

Reason	Number	Percent of Recipients	Percent of Those Removed
Moved to new district	43	13.2	42.6
Died	20	6.2	19.8
Moved to almshouse	5	1.5	5.0
Moved to Widows' Asylum	3	0.9	3.0
Fulfilled need	4	1.2	4.0
Exhibited intemperance	1	0.3	1.0
Child came of age	2	0.6	2.0
Child died	2	0.6	2.0
Removed request (later resumed)	1	0.3	1.0
Removed by committee	1	0.3	1.0
Moved to new district (later came back)	3	0.9	3.0
Unknown	16	4.9	15.8
Not off	224	68.9	
Total	325		

Source: Register of Relief Recipients, 1828–1832, vol. 2, Guardians of the Poor, Philadelphia City Archives, Philadelphia.
Note: See n. 13 to Chapter 3 for information on sample.

The first public almshouse in Philadelphia was built in 1732—sixty-eight years before the Chester County institution. The Pennsylvania Hospital (1751) and the Bettering House (1767) also accommodated some of the city's sick and able-bodied paupers.[64] As of 1800, the Bettering House and the Almshouse were converted into separate men's and women's buildings within the almshouse compound.[65] Blockley Almshouse, a bigger structure set in the more rural Blockley township, was constructed in the 1830s.[66] Philadelphia housed 788 poor individuals at public expense at the time that Chester County was opening its new poorhouse for 94 inmates.[67] Overcrowding was severe in the city institutions, with five to six beds in each ten by ten foot or eleven by eleven foot room.[68] By the year 1823, as many as 4,212 paupers strained its capacity.[69] The problem of providing for the poor had outgrown home-based aid in both Chester County and Philadelphia, but the city required a speedier solution on a larger scale.

Admissions records survive unevenly in both counties. The only extant listing of resident paupers in the Chester County poorhouse is the Admissions and Examinations Book for 1841–1851. This is equivalent to the Examination of the Paupers records in Philadelphia, which cover the period from 1822 to 1844. Both lists pertain only to legal residents applying for admission to the almshouses and, therefore, inadequately describe the institutions' populations as a whole. In the Admissions and Examinations Book, only three out of sixty-nine female paupers were identified as widows, and little was said about inmates. In Philadelphia, in contrast, the Daily Occurrence Dockets contain detailed information about the individuals admitted, including marital status. Because so little information exists for Chester County, the long-term analysis of the poor almshouse widow presented here includes only those in the Philadelphia institution.[70]

The Philadelphia almshouse records have a number of peculiarities and biases that must be taken into account when studying the lives of the people they describe. Because the poor relief system helped only the residents of a particular area, some individuals gave false names or information to protect themselves from removal to their home district. Further, the admission records, regardless of their accuracy, clearly reflect and record the values and judgments of the Overseers who kept them. Beyond these general problems of accuracy and bias are the particular difficulties involved in tracing widows through any set of records because of name changes due to marriage. The listing of marital status itself is suspect in almshouse documents: Because of the stigma attached to illegitimacy, women might name a fictitious dead husband as father of their children or an unborn child.[71] All of these factors distort the picture of the widowed woman drawn from poorhouse records, but there is still much of value in these sources.

To establish a residence in a particular community, and thus qualify for any kind of public charity (according to Pennsylvania law), an individual was required to live in a county for one year or pay taxes in that county for two consecutive years.[72] Some of the transient poor found themselves in a community in which they wanted to remain, but in which, as recent arrivals, they were ineligible for public assistance. The widow Mary Nannum, a legal resident of Delaware County, where she was raised, applied for entry into the Chester County almshouse under an assumed name in March 1844 to avoid being sent back to her native county. As the wife of a convict and the mother of four children, she spent much of her adult life moving from place to place in search of a living. This transient existence interfered with her efforts to obtain shelter at the Chester County almshouse. Finding herself pregnant, she asked for aid there under the name of Mary McBride, describing herself to the Guardians as thirty-six years old, single, and an immigrant from England. In the time required for the Guardians to check her story, she must have thought, she would give birth and recover sufficiently to leave the almshouse. Her plan went amiss in May, when someone who knew her true identity also entered the almshouse: "We yesterday admitted in a Destitute condition James Nannum a boy 7 to 9 years old; in the course of the day we found that this woman calling herself Mary McBride was the Mother of the Boy of Nannum; and the Widdow of G Washington Nannum." The Guardians wrote the next day to the Delaware County authorities, requesting directions on "how to dispose of her."[73] Although Mary Nannum was unsuccessful, other widows and relief seekers probably managed to assume false identities without being discovered.

The Guardians' reaction to paupered widows like Mary Nannum emerges in some of the vignettes that followed the basic descriptive information collected from new inmates. The widowed woman named "Fatnel" was described on entering the almshouse on 27 September 1796 as "a very hauty mischief making consequencial former Customer."[74] The same judgmental tone marked the 1801 entry for Ann Lowry. On a visit to Philadelphia, the Widow Lowry became ill, which forced her to seek refuge in the almshouse. The Overseer who admitted her showed his disdain for those who would allow a sick acquaintance to become dependent on public charity, decribing them as "friends as she stiles them."[75] Overseers also praised those widows who exhibited a proper moral character. Ann Shaffer, the young widow of Barnett Shaffer, a victim of yellow fever, was described as "very decent & well Brougt up."[76] Such details about a widow's character or condition— though reflections of the Overseers' personal views rather than precise socioeconomic data—tell us something useful about how the system worked.

Even an honestly reported name could obscure a widow's identity. Some widows failed to give their maiden name or previous married names on entering the institution; whether they felt no obligation or were not required to do so, it is clear that the records are incomplete. If Sarah Renny had not told the Overseers that on her two previous visits her name had been Sarah Davis and later Sarah Shearer, those sojourns in the poorhouse would not have been recorded on her third admission.[77] Sloppy bookkeeping may have compounded the difficulty of tracing widows through almshouse records. Maria Miller entered the almshouse in 1829 with a burned leg caused "by falling of a stove." The Overseer, baffled, wrote, "Says she was here twice before cannot find her name."[78] "Former customers," as they were often called, were probably more common, particularly among women, than the records indicate.

On the other hand, the records probably inflated the number of widows among the female population. Some women, for example, called themselves widows to cover sexual impropriety. When Rebecca Jenkins came into the almshouse pregnant, in 1821, she claimed "she was married 2 wks & her husband has been 2 wks dead & she is Pregnant by him—so she says."[79] Maria Brack, twenty-three years old, gained admittance in 1819, calling herself a widow and stating that her husband had died in the almshouse eighteen months earlier. The Overseer commented, "I can find however no demonstrable proof of this." The questionable Widow Brack was placed in the Venereal Ward.[80] The number of women who falsely identified themselves as widows simply cannot be estimated.

It must be understood that the almshouse was the place of last resort for most poor people, and in this widows were no exception. They entered the institution in desperation and left as soon as possible, and most never returned. The miserable condition in which some of the widowed inmates finally came to the almshouse demonstrates their reluctance to become a member of the dependent poor if other options were still available. Mary Allen, "a naked Distress'd rambler swarming with vermin," and Mary Keating, "poor, miserable, distressed, half starved and almost naked," and Jane Ann Smith, "poor, miserable, decrip old Woman . . . *being scarcely* able to drag one foot after the other," obviously waited to enter the poorhouse until their conditions allowed no alternative.[81] Reasons for avoiding the almshouse included the unhealthy crowded conditions and the total dependence of institutional life. On admittance, the pauper handed over the possessions she brought with her to help defray the cost of her stay. Lydia Shippler had to surrender "Eight lumps of Butter."[82] Mary Beesley, whom the cell keeper Thomas Barry had obviously searched, had "a Silver teaspoon in her pocket." It was given to the Steward.[83] The strict adherence to this policy of confiscation made any but the most desperate widow shun institutional aid. The widowed inmate used the almshouse as a place to regain her health, have a baby, obtain food and shelter during a sojourn in the city—or die. As soon as she was able, she left the institution, with or without the Overseers' permission. The squalor, disease, and dehumanization she encountered there usually ensured that the widow would not willingly return, and most poor widows who entered the Philadelphia poorhouse during the time under study did so only once.[84]

Under such conditions, widows were until 1828 a small fraction of the overall almshouse population. In 1813, when the administrators began to keep statistics of the population by gender, widowed inmates averaged only 2 percent of the institution's female adult population.[85] Despite a small rise in the number of widows during the depression of 1819, for most of the period between 1813 and 1827 widows represented less than 5 percent of the female almshouse population. After 1828, the proportion of widows exploded to over 20 percent and continued to rise. Priscilla Clement has argued, looking at aggregate almshouse population figures by gender, that the elimination of outdoor relief in 1828 did not cause former pensioners to resort to institutional life.[86] When the records are examined with an eye to marital status, however, it is clear that the 1828 Poor Law did in fact have a devastating impact on widowed pensioners who, without a weekly dole, were forced to enter the almshouse. Most widows had avoided residence in the poorhouse by patching together an income from a variety of sources. This precarious existence could not accommodate the sudden removal of a steady dole of fifty cents. The loss of outdoor relief thrust many over the edge into institutionalization.

Although outdoor relief widows swelled the almshouse cohort after 1828, the widowed inmates of the Philadelphia institution, in general, differed somewhat from their counterparts in the "outdoor" population. The typical widow in the almshouse had lived in the poorest sections of the city and was an immigrant, most likely a native of Ireland (Table 3-7). She was between thirty and thirty-nine years old. She came into the institution because of ill health as well as poverty.

The widows residing in the almshouse came from the city proper or Southwark—rarely from the northern outskirts of the county, where the outdoor relief widow was most likely to reside (Table 3-8). Most characteristically, these women lived near the docks or in the many alleyways and back streets of the poorer portions of the city. Many lived a beggar's existence, without a permanent place of

TABLE 3-7
Place of Birth for Widows in the Philadelphia Almshouse,
1789–1834

Birthplace	Number	Percent
PENNSYLVANIA (27.9%)		
Philadelphia	472	20.9
Surrounding counties	102	4.5
Other Pennsylvania	57	2.5
SURROUNDING STATES (20.8%)		
New Jersey	169	7.5
Delaware	175	7.8
New York	35	1.6
Maryland	89	3.9
OTHER STATES (2.8%)		
District of Columbia	1	0
North Carolina	7	0.3
New England	2	0.1
Kentucky	2	0.1
Virginia	31	1.4
U.S.	1	0
Massachusetts	9	0.4
Washington City	1	0
Ohio	2	0.1
Rhode Island	2	0.1
Connecticut	3	0.1
South Carolina	3	0.1
Georgia	1	0
Carolina	1	0
Maine	2	0.1
New Hampshire	1	0
EUROPE (38.9%)		
Ireland	641	28.4
England	101	4.5
Scotland	22	1.0
Wales	2	0.1
Germany	77	3.4
Switzerland	1	0

Continued on next page

Table 3-7—Continued

France	14	0.6
Holland	18	0.8
Sweden	2	0.1
Bavaria	1	0
OTHER (1.3%)		
Canada	3	0.1
East Indies	1	0
Bermuda	2	0.1
Africa	3	0.1
West Indies	5	0.2
Santa Cruz	1	0
St. Kitts	2	0.1
Isle of Guernsey	1	0
St. Domingo	1	0
At sea	15	0.7
UNKNOWN	175	7.8
Total	2,256	

Source: Daily Occurrence Dockets, Guardians of the Poor, 1789–1834, Philadelphia City Archives, Philadelphia.
Note: See n. 70 to Chapter 3 for study population.

residence, before desperation forced them to take refuge in the poorhouse. The seasonal pattern of admissions into the institution, furthermore, suggests that cold weather forced widows living on the streets to seek shelter (Table 3-9).[87] A visitor to the Chester County almshouse in 1842 condescendingly described the kind of "idle [paupers], who in the autumn and beginning of Winter obtrude themselves into the house to lounge away the winter season."[88] The winter weather also forced widows like Ann Kyle, a twenty-five-year-old mother of two, to ask the Philadelphia Overseers for shelter from the cold. She had "no legal settlement except it be in New York, her husband died 3 weeks ago at Harrisburgh, she is on her way to New York, but unable to proceed on account of the cold."[89]

TABLE 3-8
District of Residence for Widows in the Philadelphia Almshouse,
1789–1834

District	Number	Percent	District Population as Percent of City Total[a] 1790	1830
City	1,140	50.5	63.6	53.0
Southward	586	26.0	12.6	13.7
Northern Liberties	195	8.6	22.1	20.7
Kensington	36	1.6	0	8.8
Penn Township	63	2.8	0	1.7
Roxborough	1	0	1.7	2.2
Unknown	235	10.4		
Total	2,256			

Source: Daily Occurrence Dockets, Guardians of the Poor, 1789–1834, Philadelphia City Archives, Philadelphia.
Note: See n. 70 to Chapter 3 for study population.
   [a] Based on 1790 and 1830 censuses. Census figures were taken from John Daly and Allen Weinberg, *Genealogy of Philadelphia County Subdivisions* (Philadelphia: City of Philadelphia, Department of Records, 1975), 93.

This population of institutionalized women was also relatively young (Table 3-10). Widowed inmates in the Philadelphia almshouse were overwhelmingly between twenty and forty-nine (61.8 percent). Outdoor relief paupers, in contrast, were on the whole over sixty (75.9 percent). The poorhouse population is usually characterized as elderly, and there is some basis for this view in other areas. Susan Grigg found that in Newburyport widows over sixty made up two-thirds of the widowed almshouse residents. She suggests that as a widow became older, she tended to slip from the ranks of the independent paupers on outdoor relief to the dependency of the poorhouse.[90] The reverse was the case in Philadelphia: the young and

TABLE 3-9
Month of Admittance for Widows in the Philadelphia
Almshouse, 1789–1834

Month	Number	Percent
January	207	9.2
February	165	7.3
March	159	7.0
April	142	6.3
May	173	7.7
June	141	6.3
July	154	6.8
August	172	7.6
September	203	9.0
October	209	9.3
November	265	11.7
December	263	11.7
Unknown	3	0.1
Total	2,256	

Source: Daily Occurrence Dockets, Guardians of the Poor, 1789–1834, Philadelphia City Archives, Philadelphia.
Note: See n. 70 to Chapter 3 for study propulation.

middle-aged were in the almshouse, and the old were on outdoor relief. One can speculate that the Overseers chose to provide older widowed residents with assistance at home, while giving young widows temporary shelter and food only within an institution in order to discourage idleness.

Many widows sought residence in the almshouse because, as Mary Allen admitted in 1800, they were "very sick and weak indeed, with the companion poverty."[91] Although many widows simply attributed their poverty to some temporary illness (43.7 percent of the total admitted, 50.7 percent of those giving any reason at all), about half

TABLE 3-10
Age of Widows in the Philadelphia Almshouse, 1789–1834

Age	Number	Percent
15–19	24	1.1
20–29	415	18.4
30–39	572	25.4
40–49	405	18.0
50–59	325	14.4
60–69	208	9.2
70–79	109	4.8
80–89	43	1.9
90–100	17	0.8
Unknown	138	6.1
Total	2,256	

Source: Daily Occurrence Dockets, Guardians of the Poor, 1789–1834, Philadelphia City Archives, Philadelphia.
Note: See n. 70 to Chapter 3 for study population.

of the women citing a reason for their destitution named other causes (Table 3-11): Intemperance, injury, small children, and pregnancy each reduced a substantial number of widowed women to the dependent poverty of the almshouse. But reasons of this sort were likely to draw less sympathy and consequently less aid from charitable strangers, or even the Overseers, than would illness in an elderly widow.

The chronically poor, labeled "former customers," entered the institution as many as twenty-five times. They usually came in with recurring complaints of venereal disease, intemperance, rheumatism, insurmountable poverty, or other ills. Most of these widows lived in the slums of Southwark, coming to the poorhouse when life outside, particularly in the winter, became too onerous. The un-

TABLE 3-11
Reasons for Poverty for Widows in the Philadelphia Almshouse,
1789–1834

Reason	Number	Percent	Percent of Those Listing a Reason
Sickness	985	39.5	50.7
Injury	149	6.0	7.7
Pregnancy	143	5.7	7.4
Rheumatism	134	5.4	6.9
Mental illness	69	2.8	3.6
Intemperance	161	6.5	8.3
Venereal disease	50	2.0	2.6
Drug addiction	8	0.3	0.4
Young children	67	2.7	3.4
Children who cannot help	1	0	0
Inability to work	72	2.9	3.7
Poverty	71	2.8	3.7
Old age	17	0.7	0.9
No friends	14	0.6	0.7
Low pay	1	0	0
Husband's misfortunes	1	0	0
Known reason	1,943		
No reason listed	550		
Total	2,493		

Source: Daily Occurrence Dockets, Guardians of the Poor, 1789–1834, Philadelphia City Archives, Philadelphia.
Note: See n. 70 to Chapter 3 for study population. Of the 2,256 cases, some widows had more than one reason for poverty. Each reason was counted separately.

sympathetic Overseers usually consigned them to the Cells in the basement of the almshouse. Catharine Blight, described as "an elderly woman," gained admittance into the almshouse on 1 June 1801, having previously entered on 21 April and 26 May of the same year.

Is come in now with a bottle of spirituous liquor, and highly
intoxicated for which reason she was conducted to one of the
Cells, there to remain till she gets sober; at the same time
she gave to Elira Connec an old red Morocco Pocket-book.
containing three five dollar Notes of the Bank of Pennsylvania.
one Quarter and three sixteenths of a dollar in Silver, one and
a half cents and a pair of scissors, and some sewingthread. all
of which were by order of the Managers put into the hands of
the Steward.[92]

About a month later the Widow Blight tired of her confinement and her limited supply of alcohol and "eloped" from
the institution.[93] Betsy Curry, after fifteen visits to the
almshouse, knew something about the system and tried to
get the best treatment. When she came into the poorhouse
on 1 October 1832, she complained of illness and was sent
to the the Medical Ward, where the real reason for her
debility was uncovered. "Word has just been sent in that
instead of being sick she is under the influence of L'eau de
Vie, her destination of course is changed. to the *Cells*."[94]

For black women, additionally burdened by racial dis-
crimination, poverty was often more severe and options
more limited. Twenty-six widows were listed in the 1837
census of black paupers in the Philadelphia almshouse. Of
these women, 54 percent (14 out of 26) did housework, 12
percent (3) were cooks, one woman described herself as a
"market woman," and 31 percent (8) gave no occupation.[95]
These widows, like black women in the city as a whole,
overwhelmingly performed low-paying, unskilled domestic
work.[96] The black widow rarely received outdoor relief to
supplement her low wages. Only 2.5 percent (8 out of 325)
of widows on outdoor relief between 1828 and 1832 were
black, and they received less than their white counterparts:

thirty-eight cents as opposed to fifty cents a week, on the average. Black or mulatto women constituted 12.3 percent (278 out of 2,256) of the widowed population in the Philadelphia almshouse between 1789 and 1834. When things went wrong for her, the poor black widow, in a low-paying job with limited access to supplemental income from outdoor charity, often had to accept the inevitability of institutional life.

The average widow in the almshouse was, in sum, a young woman drawn to the city by the promise of opportunity and finding instead poverty and despair. Many historians have identified the urban environment as a magnet for young women searching for employment.[97] Some of the less successful jobseekers found themselves in the almshouse. Chronically poor widows used it as a temporary shelter when life on the street became difficult. On the whole, however, poor widowed women avoided this dreaded institution with the help of outdoor relief. Moreover, the poverty of widowhood represented for most not a dramatic reversal of fortune but a slip from the marginal existence she had known as a poor wife. Left to fend for herself after her husband's death, she continued to work and pursued other sources of income. Her situation was precarious, and any mischance could lead to economic disaster and dependence on institutional aid. Yet most poor widows, through experience, good health, and skill—and perhaps some good fortune as well—apparently escaped the specter of dependent poverty.

Like her poorer counterpart, the widow of means had to find some new balance of work and income to support herself and any children she had. Her greater resources, however, tended to leave her well beyond an elemental struggle for freedom from institutionalization. Even more

than those resourceful women of scant means who managed to stay out of the almshouse, widows who enjoyed the
opportunity to go beyond mere subsistence illustrate how
early American women coped outside the domestic "woman's sphere."

4

A "Man of Business": The Widow of Means

Widows left with adequate resources often managed to maintain or even improve their financial circumstances. Probate records and other manuscript sources reveal that a widowed woman's economic activities could involve much more than collecting an annuity or firewood from a reluctant relative. Widows ran their deceased husbands' shops in Philadelphia, took over their husbands' farms in Chester County, and even created new sources of income unrelated to their former spouses' occupations. And many widows, even when left in easy circumstances, strove to improve their standard of living with the resources at hand rather than accept their inheritance and live in retirement. Many women died owning more property than they inherited. The experience and behavior of this active, better-off group of widows support the conclusion that economic decline was not a fate that all widowed women shared.[1]

Pennsylvania inheritance law did little to guarantee a widow an adequate income. As Marylynn Salmon has shown, a widow's claim under Pennsylvania law was less important than a creditor's. Unlike most other American colonies, which assured a woman at least a life interest in one-third of her husband's real estate, Pennsylvania made even this portion vulnerable to creditors. A widow could lose her entire inheritance if her husband's estate owed sufficient debts. This, Salmon concludes, constituted a special hardship for Pennsylvania widows: The law in effect made the wife liable for her husband's debts though unable to prevent their accumulation.[2] Yet the clear evidence of widows' competence in handling executorial responsibility raises questions about the scope of female initiative within marriage. The fact that both marriage partners were liable may have encouraged women to be more informed about their husbands' financial circumstances.

Inheritance law did not reflect the subtle but significant changes of custom that occurred in the late eighteenth and early nineteenth centuries. Most men who wrote wills, for example, were more generous to their widows than Pennsylvania law required, and those in Philadelphia and Chester County left their wives more than the traditional one-third of their property. Other studies have found a similar pattern in early Bucks County, Pennsylvania, in Virginia, and in Massachusetts.[3] Even when creditors' rights left some widows with far less than their specified share, the terms stipulated in these wills reveal the positive, creative intentions of the men who wrote them. The fact that a husband wrote a will seems in itself to indicate a dissatisfaction with Pennsylvania's prescribed intestate proceedings, and the wills indicate a less restrictive cultural attitude toward the rights of widows than the statutes do.

Even so, the time involved in settling an estate could leave a potentially wealthy woman penniless. Katherine Banning Chew was the widow of the successful Philadelphia lawyer Benjamin Chew, Jr. According to his will, proved in 1844, she was to receive the sizeable Germantown estate known as Cliveden as well as an annuity of $2,250. Instead, a family squabble kept her dependent on the kindness of her children. She wrote many letters to her daughter Anne, begging for financial assistance.

> I am so much in want of some money to pay for *my* necessaries that I must again entreat that a remittance be made immediately—I have offers for my Maryland *Lots* &—I think (unwillingly) that I must [illegible] sacrifice my own *Patrimony*!!!. If you have any thing to send me (even small) or anything from my *best* of Children *dearest Eliza* [another daughter], you can put in the hand of my messenger.[4]

The occasional aid Katherine Chew received from her children, together with her patrimony, provided her with a cushion against immediate economic disaster. Nevertheless, in 1852, eight years after her husband's death and three years before her own, the Widow Chew was still in court trying to extract part of her inheritance from her husband's reluctant executors.

Catharine Gibb's inheritance should have made her comfortable, but even her husband's debt-free estate gave this Chester County widow no guarantee of an adequate income. She appeared in the Chester County Orphans Court on 20 June 1780.

> That five Years past Her Husband James Gibb Departed this Life Leaving an Unencumbered Estate; out of Which your Petitioner Presumes the Laws of her Country have made provision for the widow & Children; no part of which Either Real or Personal She hath Received But hath Been Driven from her hard Earned Residence to seek her Bread. That your

> Petitioner after a Residence of more than forty years in Labour
> & Industry had flattered herself with the Devine assistance
> to Be Enabled (from her share of the said Inincumbered Estate
> to have comfortably subsisted the Remainder of her short
> span of Life) Being now upwards of Sixty Years of Age) free
> from toils ill suited to her Age & Many Infirmities.[5]

Her son controlled his father's estate and refused to make
the needed division. The widow's share was her right, on
the basis of legal precedent as well as the contribution her
labor had made to the value of the estate. She knew her
husband had left no debts; she understood what her proper
portion should be; and she felt her hard work had entitled
her to this share. Yet forty years of "Labour & Industry"
had given her nothing to prevent continued drudgery in her
old age. Her son and the slow-moving legal system combined to deny her a rightful share of the estate she had
helped build. The records are silent about whether she ever
received her due.

The law, a husband's provisions, and—in some cases—
the workings of the court system could either singly or in
combination affect the widow's economic circumstances.
Yet while the laws relating to dower rights and the court's
implementation of these laws remained relatively constant
in Pennsylvania up to the Married Women's Property Act
of 1848, an examination of wills in Philadelphia and Chester County suggests that inheritance patterns were in fact
changing along with social values.[6]

A widow's portion, in wills written in Philadelphia and
Chester County between 1750 and 1850, varied over time
and according to rural or urban residence.[7] Although a
large percentage of men in each area left idiosyncratic
legacies that fit into no discernible pattern, certain types

of bequests were made commonly enough to merit measurement. This analysis focuses on those components of wills most directly connected to the widow's economic circumstances and options. The amount and the form of her inheritance as well as her disposition of it tell us a great deal about the options open to widows and the ways they used their opportunities.

The widow's share in Chester County reflected the rural character of the region. Men who specified an occupation in their wills often called themselves yeomen (77.5 percent). Lucy Simler's work on bi-occupationalism in Chester County, has shown that "yeoman" was basically a generic term that often encompassed more than agrarian pursuits. Most such men, though, spent at least some of their time in agricultural activity.[8] Appropriately, in rural Chester County the most common pattern of bequest assured a widow maintenance in a society where land produced income. She received part of the house to live in and produce from the farm (Table 4-1).

When a man left his widow part of a farmhouse and supplies, he generally spelled out her rights in detail. In a will proved in 1820, Richard Downing of East Caln gave his wife, Elizabeth, specific provisions that their son William, who inherited the main house and farm, was expected to furnish.

Also I order my son Wm Downing to provide to my wife Hay of Good Quality & good order & put it in her stable loft, sufficient for two Cows & one Horse & a friends Creature when any such should call to see her Annually and my wifes Cattle shall always in Pasture Season pasture with my Son Wm's Cattle & be turn'd out and brought up with his Cattle during the Pasture Season, Also my son Wm shall furnish my

TABLE 4-1
**Types of Legacies Left to Widows in Philadelphia and
Chester County, 1750–1850**

Date	House and Supplies (%)	Entire Estate (%)	Idiosyncratic[a] (%)	Total Cases
CHESTER COUNTY				
1750–1759	25.0	6.8	68.2	44
1760–1769	37.7	3.3	59.0	61
1770–1779	28.6	5.4	66.0	56
1780–1789	30.2	11.1	58.7	63
1790–1799	31.4	7.8	60.8	51
1800–1809	25.5	9.8	64.7	51
1810–1819	31.3	10.4	58.3	67
1820–1829	41.4	20.7	37.9	87
1830–1839	16.2	25.0	58.8	68
1840–1850	16.5	19.8	63.7	91
Total				639
PHILADELPHIA				
1750–1759	0	21.4	78.6	14
1760–1769	0	18.8	81.2	16
1770–1779	7.7	0	92.3	13
1780–1789	9.1	13.6	77.3	22
1790–1799	0	22.2	77.8	27
1800–1809	0	43.5	56.5	23
1810–1819	3.0	36.4	60.6	33
1820–1829	0	47.2	52.8	36
1830–1839	2.3	29.5	68.2	44
1840–1850	0	49.1	50.9	57
Total				285

Sources: Chester County Wills and Administrations, Chester County Archives, West Chester; Philadelphia Wills, Register of Wills, Philadelphia.

[a] Although idiosyncratic provisions for a wife were most common in both Philadelphia and Chester County (bequests ranging from a sum of money or specific personal property to a few acres of land), this table focuses on the discernible and consistent patterns in the construction of a widow's legacy.

wife with Two Fat Hogs that shall weigh at least Two Hundred & fifty pounds each every year & a side of good Beef not less than Three Hundred pounds also Ten Bushels Potatoes, Six Hundred good flour, Sixty Single Bushels of shorts, Fifteen Bushels of Oates, Three Bushels Indian corn in ear & Three Bushels Shelld, Three Bushels Rie & Three Bushels Buckwheat.

In addition, she was to receive produce from the garden and orchard, three bushels of turnips a year, a horse, two cows, firewood, and screening to help maintain her chicken coop.[9] Similar wills frequently specify which rooms a widow could live in, use, or pass through. An almost absurdly specific example is the will of Frederick Dallman, proved in 1793. In addition to the use of a bedroom, the cellar, the kitchen, and the yard, he gave his wife "also the Occasional use of the necessary house or Privy and liberty of pasture to and from the same."[10]

Several authors have seen such provisions as products of a patriarchal family system that manipulated the lives of both widows and children. As land became scarce in eighteenth-century America, so the reasoning goes, the farm increasingly went to a single heir, who was burdened with supporting the widow.[11] In reality, inheritance patterns in Chester County reflect a more complex and equitable situation. The family farm was both a home *and* a business.[12] Many wills refer to family loyalty and affection, but also attend to the more practical matters entailed in the continued successful management of an agricultural enterprise. In several ways the usual rural widow's legacy was a common sense response to an environment where comfort, security, and the realization of family goals required both land and the labor necessary to extract a profit from it.

A tenant, moreover, could provide the labor to make a farm productive as readily as an adult child. George Smedley in 1765 made precisely this practical arrangement for his wife and minor children.

> And moreover it is my will that my Executor let my Plantation to some orderly Person or Persons that shall be bound to keep a riding Creature and Cow for my wife and to bring and take them to the field when she shall have occasion for them & Cut & bring her fire wood to or near the Door and all her Priviledges before mentioned in this will shall be Reserved to her in the Lease nor any *waist* be committed by any Tenant in any shape untill my Sons arrives to the age of twenty one.[13]

Leonard Walker provided similarly for his wife in 1825 when he secured her "the choice of a tenant" as well as the right to show him which wood he could take "off of the place" as his three-cord yearly portion.[14] Given the numerous tenants found by Simler in Chester County, this nonfamilial, businesslike exchange was an effective and viable way for a widow to profit from her farm.[15]

Even the familiar arrangement in which mother and son shared a property did not always force the widow to wait for her son to deliver the appropriate goods, or to hope he would permit her to use the privy. John Dicky described in his will of 1797 a business partnership between his wife and son, both of whom were named executors of his estate.

> My desire is that my executors together—where we now Dwell and manage the farm as heretofore usually Done by me and that the[e] and each of them share equally and alike in all the profits and issues ariseing or made from or out of my said farm and that each of them bear a proportional and equal part

in all expences and charges requisite or necessary for manage-ing the same.[16]

This widow-and-son team ran the family agricultural busi-ness together, sharing equally in the profits and losses of the enterprise; in fact, their joint involvement in the farm may have begun before the writing of John's will.

Just as shared living space had business as well as familial purposes, the detailed list of supplies allotted to a widow was more than a guarantee against a slothful son and starvation. Tenants, not just offspring, were made re-sponsible for providing the widow with firewood and food-stuffs. And the large quantity of farm produce given to the widow frequently provided her with resources well beyond a mere subsistence. Bettye Hobbs Pruitt has already ques-tioned whether the widow's portion was intended to pro-vide her simply with necessities. She argues that some of these supplies were a surplus designed to sell on the mar-ket.[17] For Chester County at the end of the eighteenth century, James Lemon estimates that a widow received, on average, a bequest of 13.2 bushels of wheat per year.[18] Pruitt calculated that this would amount to two pounds of wheat bread or 2,300 calories per day, 61 percent of the necessary caloric intake for a modern-day active woman weighing 138 pounds. Given the overall health of the colonial Amer-ican population and the probability that a woman con-sumed other starches, such a diet seems unlikely.[19] In short, she was left more wheat than she needed. Some men, like Richard Downing of East Caln, who left his wife "six Hundred [bushels] good flour," clearly bequeathed an amount that can only be interpreted as a surplus intended for sale. These extra quantities of grain or other farm produce afforded the widow some flexibility in obtaining goods and services she needed or wanted. A roof over her head and food were only part of what the widow required to live comfortably. Produce was part of the income of the family agricultural business. By bequeathing generous amounts of farm goods to his wife, a husband in effect provided her with the means for arranging her material life according to her own judgment.

A legacy of farm produce also allowed a rural widow some protection against the economic fluctuations common in late eighteenth- and early nineteenth-century America. Such a bequest sheltered her from inflation better than a cash annuity, which could lose real value. Conversely, in times of depression when prices were low, she had food even if she encountered difficulties in selling the excess for profit. An ample portion also protected her from the repercussions of a bad farming season. An astute, caring Chester County farmer was probably less concerned about who worked his farm, or the minimum standard of nourishment for his wife, than about his farm's remaining a viable business to provide his widow with comfort, security, and perhaps a tidy profit.

The Chester County farmer who willed part of his house and supplies to his wife took reasonable, not just conventional, measures to ensure her economic survival in an agricultural community. She lived on the farm with her minor children, if she had any, and an adult child or tenant. This arrangement provided her with a business and the requisite labor to make it profitable. The widow received her set part of the final product, which she then could consume or sell as she saw fit. Although this type of inheritance had familial implications, the testator's intentions were probably less patriarchal than economically practical.

The chiefly practical nature of the typical Chester County legacy is underlined by the change in inheritance patterns that occurred between 1750 and 1850 in this predominantly rural area (Table 4-1). The two decades after 1830 witnessed a significant drop in bequests of house and supplies (16.2 and 16.5 percent of all wills) and a rise in the percentage of widows who were left an entire estate (19.8 and 25.0 percent).[20] This shift reflects the changing nature of that agricultural community.[21] As small towns grew among the homesteads in the nineteenth century, more men made their living away from the farm. The small shopkeeper or blacksmith living in West Chester was less likely to provide his wife with a farmhouse and supplies of grain and produce. This decline in bequests of house and supplies made Chester County inheritance patterns much more like those in Philadelphia, where farm ownership was rare. In providing for their widows in a rather different way, men were adapting to new economic realities.

As was true of wills leaving house and supplies, executorial assignments that might seem to limit the options of a Chester County widow in fact were reflective of the economic environment in which the testator's family would have to function. There was a trend in married men's wills, as the nineteenth century progressed, toward appointing someone other than one's wife as executor (Tables 4-2 and 4-3).[22] This was clearly only a rural pattern. In a farming community where land was becoming less plentiful, there was a need to consolidate the estate in the hands of a single beneficiary if a family was to maintain its standard of living after the death of a husband and father. That the owner of the farm should be the one to collect the debts and pay the creditors was a sound business judgment.[23]

TABLE 4-2
Widows as Executors in Chester County, 1750–1850

Years	Sole		With Others		Excluded		Total
	Number	Percent	Number	Percent	Number	Percent	
1750–1759	6	13.6	25	56.8	13	29.5	44
1760–1769	8	13.1	31	50.8	22	36.1	61
1770–1779	7	12.5	24	42.9	25	44.6	56
1780–1789	6	9.5	29	46.0	28	44.4	63
1790–1799	3	5.9	16	31.4	32	62.7	51
1800–1809	2	3.9	21	41.2	28	54.9	51
1810–1819	4	6.0	25	37.3	38	56.7	67
1820–1829	7	8.0	19	21.8	61	70.1	87
1830–1839	5	7.4	11	16.2	52	76.5	68
1840–1850	15	16.5	24	26.4	52	57.1	91
Total	63	9.9	225	35.2	351	54.9	639

Source: Chester County Wills and Administrations, Chester County Archives, West Chester.

Note: This table is based on a sample of wills probated from 1749/50 through 1850. Only men who mentioned a living spouse in their wills are included. A 20 percent sample was taken because the decedent population in Chester County was (incorrectly) expected to be smaller than that in Philadelphia. Residents of the area that became Delaware County (in 1789) are included.

The situation in Philadelphia was different, but legacies were comparable in spirit. Philadelphia men tended to provide their widows with an inheritance that suited the economic life of the city. Most urban husbands who wrote wills were craftsmen, shopkeepers, or merchants (Table 4-4). They left their wives annuities, interest from stocks and bonds, personal property, and real estate (both investment and residential), but only very rarely part of a house and supplies. That kind of inheritance was inappropriate in a rapidly expanding urban economy. In fact, as Philadelphia became more industrialized, testators increasingly chose to leave their entire estates to their wives. The

TABLE 4-3
Widows as Executors in Philadelphia, 1750–1850

Years	Sole		With Others		Excluded		Total
	Number	Percent	Number	Percent	Number	Percent	
1750–1759	5	35.7	5	35.7	4	28.6	14
1760–1769	4	25.0	7	43.8	5	31.3	16
1770–1779	1	7.7	7	53.8	5	38.5	13
1780–1789	4	18.2	12	54.5	6	27.3	22
1790–1799	4	14.8	12	44.4	11	40.7	27
1800–1809	5	21.7	15	65.2	3	13.0	23
1810–1819	8	24.2	16	48.5	9	27.3	33
1820–1829	14	38.9	15	41.7	7	19.4	36
1830–1839	12	27.3	15	34.1	17	38.6	44
1840–1850	10	17.5	16	28.1	31	54.4	57
Total	67	23.5	120	42.1	98	34.4	285

Source: Philadelphia Wills, Register of Wills, Philadelphia.
Note: This table is based on a sample of wills probated from 1749/50 through 1850. Only men who mentioned a living spouse in their wills are included. A 10 percent sample was taken. Residents of the area outside the modern boundaries of the city (that is, Montgomery County) are excluded in order to keep the group primarily urban and yet still include other areas of the county that were really part of the urban environment by 1850.

custom of giving a widow everything became so prevalent that after 1800 almost half (41 percent) of all married testators from the city provided their widows with this type of legacy, in contrast to less than a seventh (under 14 percent) for the years 1750 to 1790. What accounts for the increasing occurrence of this pattern in Philadelphia and Chester County after 1830? There are several factors that might, in an increasingly market-driven, urban-industrial environment, make it desirable to give everything to one's wife.

A married couple formed an economic unit, and both partners worked to promote its financial well-being. The

TABLE 4-4
**Class Divisions Based on Occupation for Husbands Who Left
Wills in Philadelphia, 1750–1850**

Occupation and Class[a]	Number
UPPER (23.0% OF THOSE LISTING OCCUPATION)	
Merchants	23
Professionals	5
Titled	13
Manufacturers	2
MIDDLING GROUPS (49.7%)	
Wood crafts	23
Metal crafts	14
Leather crafts	6
Textile crafts	10
Other crafts	18
White-collar	1
Captains	—
Shopkeepers	21
LOWER SORT (11.8%)	22
(Mariner, carter, stevedore, laborer, waiter, porter)	
UNSPECIFIED (15.5%)	29
(Yeoman, husbandman, farmer, planter, freeholder)	
Total known occupation	187
NONE LISTED	98
Total	285

Source: Philadelphia Wills, Register of Wills, Philadelphia.

[a] These occupational categories and class divisions are based on those in Susan Edith Klepp, "Philadelphia in Transition: A Demographic History of the City and Its Occupational Groups, 1720–1830" (Ph.D. dissertation, University of Pennsylvania, 1980), 329–331. The unspecified group of occupations that have an ambiguous relationship to class, and a few specific occupations not included by Klepp, were adopted from the appendix to Gary B. Nash, *The Urban Crucible: Social Change, Political Consciousness, and the Origins of the American Revolution* (Cambridge: Harvard University Press, 1979), 387–391, table 1.

economic success of the family, furthermore, whether on the farm or in the city, often required considerably more from a woman than the mastery of domestic chores. It is apparent that a wife often functioned as a silent partner in her husband's business. Even if the family had great wealth, the wife frequently understood the investment process and knew the full extent of the family's holdings. Widows' behavior gives us good reason to believe that these women were familiar with the economic affairs of their families before their husbands' deaths.

The men who entrusted their widows with their entire estates were most often middle-level craftsmen and shopkeepers. The widow who inherited a drygoods store or tailor's shop simply continued to run the enterprise after her husband's death for the benefit of the family. Claudia Goldin has examined the frequency with which Philadelphia widows between 1800 and 1860 took over their husbands' shops and businesses. Using city directories and census data, she concludes that a large portion of the widows in her sample followed the careers of their deceased husbands. Women were particularly likely to keep their spouses' shops, grocery stores, and other small businesses operating.[24] Middle-income testators bequeathed everything to their widows because they valued their wives' business sense. This trust almost certainly grew from years of working together behind the store counter.[25]

Wills refer directly to the wife's integral role in a family-run enterprise. Thomas Bryan, a cabinetmaker in the city, wrote his will in June 1799, a month before his death. To provide for his widow and six children, he left his shop to both his wife and son. "I will & direct that the said benches & tools shall be still kept & used by him [his son] in carrying on the trade & business jointly with his mother for the better support & bringing up of my younger children." This arrangement would remain in effect until his youngest daughter turned sixteen, "& for such longer time as they my said wife & [son] can mutually agree."[26] Thomas Bryan left his family a business to support them. His widow and son, as he and his wife had done, would run the business for the good of the family. Bryan had, incidentally, no illusions that this partnership would always progress smoothly, but he saw the continued success of the family enterprise as the overriding interest for all.

John Stroup, who died in 1825, had a provision in his will that would have hurt his widow financially if she decided not to continue his tailoring business. "I will that if my wife should not be willing to follow my business that my shop goods shall be praised and my son John shall have them at the appraisement if he will except of it."[27] This testator not only expected his wife to run his shop; he made it undesirable for her to do otherwise.

Just as widows of moderate means understood the workings of their husbands' shops, truly wealthy widows knew the nature of their material assets and how to use them effectively. It seems unlikely that they suddenly acquired this capacity after bereavement. In their letters and diaries, affluent women demonstrate familiarity with real estate values, the nuances of stock investments, and even subtle indicators of change in the economy. Some wealthy men were willing to acquaint their wives with the family finances and the condition of their businesses. Not surprisingly, when their spouses passed away, many of these women had little trouble in making the transition to financial managers. Elizabeth Powel, the widow of Samuel Powel, one of the wealthiest men in Philadelphia, stated her economic philosophy in a letter to a tenant delinquent

with his rent. "Every Man of business must be sensible,—
that if I wish to preserve integrity in my own engagements
I take care that others are punctual in their payments to
me."[28] Like her husband, she thought of herself as a "man
of business."

Elizabeth Powel was familiar with property values beyond her own real estate investments. She not only understood the net worth of her own land, but in a more general
way knew what made some properties more valuable than
others. Her nephew, John Hare Powel, solicited her advice
on a real estate acquisition in 1809. Her detailed response
demonstrates her knowledge of the subtleties of the real
estate market.

> I have most seriously reflected on your proposal respecting
> the purchase of Mr Binghams Estate in the vicinity of Powel-
> ton [her home], and am of the opinion, that it would eventu-
> ally prove a very bad speculation—The front on the old Lan-
> caster Road is very small—not more than four Acres, and even
> that will I believe be very soon lessened by a publick Road
> that is at this Moment intended to be run at the West end of
> Powelton. It is a large Tract of at least One hundred Acres—
> the Land bad,—broken and generally uncultivated, worn out
> and has never by Mr. Bingham been replenished with Stable
> or other Manure—it is remote from the Roads on which
> improvements are at present contemplated—no Title can be
> made under existing Circumstances that would not subject
> the Purchasers to vexations contingencies such as would
> probably defeat the best concerted Plans that could be devised
> for either emolument or pleasure. If it was in my offer tomor-
> row at $200—per Acre unencumbered (as it now is with a
> minority of thirteen Years which may be protracted without
> end should Wm Bingham have a child under age and die
> himself in his minority) I would reject the offer.[29]

In this letter, as in much of her correspondence, the Widow Powel displayed her thorough knowledge of investment strategy. She knew the effect a public road would have on a property, the importance of replenishing farm land, and the intricacies of inheritance law. Certainly her economic acumen rivaled that of many men of the period.

Similar knowledge of the volatility of the real estate market helped Mary Parker Norris, second wife and widow of Charles Norris, plan her property dealings. When Congress chose not to return to Philadelphia in 1785, she wrote to her son about her thwarted plan to take advantage of the formerly booming real estate market.

> If Congress had returned to Philada., I believe I should have let the Mansion I reside in to the Dutch Minister, he wanted the house, and if I could have had a good rent should have let it, as it is much too large for me, but that prospect is now at an end, for the presant however, and house-rent lower, & it is thought will yet fall.[30]

Instead of settling for an inferior rent, she chose to wait for the market to change. A true understanding of real estate values involved knowing when to rent and when to sell, and when to do neither. Mary Norris reminded her married daughter of the need to weigh these options carefully before selling part of her partrimony: "I do hope if thee sells thy Lot in the Court that thee will not let it go at a low price, Land now Sells very high everywhere, consider whither it would be best for thyself to sell, or let on Groundrent."[31] Clearly such matters were considered appropriate concerns of women.

The shrewd Elizabeth Powel manipulated her investments according to her personal evaluation of the fluctuating antebellum economy. As we have seen, she sold her stock in the Bank of the United States against the advice of her nephew and her lawyer. She sold her thirty shares "at 10 per cent advance dividend off—which I consider as good as 14 per cent." Anxious to finalize the deal, she asked her nephew to make the transfer for her the next day. She was gambling that the bank's charter would not be renewed and wanted "the business completed tomorrow before the decision of Congress can be known here."[32] This businesswoman showed better intuition than the two men who advised her. In the uncertain years before the War of 1812, the Widow Powel was acutely aware of the need to protect her investments. She explained her strategy to a neighbor in August 1811: "The primary object contemplated by me in the investment of monies . . . [is] placing personal Estate on a more permanent Base in the present fluctuating state of our public affairs."[33] She obviously knew that real estate held its value during an economic crisis better than stocks and bonds. Elizabeth Powel managed to maintain her estate and die a very wealthy woman. At her death in 1830, her personal estate alone was worth $141,573.47.

The evidence in Philadelphia suggests that men often trusted their wives' economic skills and that women deserved this confidence. In these middle- and upper-class families, labor and financial information were shared. In marriage and after its dissolution by death, the economic well-being of the family was the goal. While her husband was alive, the wife's contribution was unpaid labor at the store or possibly her opinion about investment strategy. When the husband faced death, this intimate business relationship of marriage partners, unencumbered by the constraints of agricultural production, was reflected in a generous bequest to the wife. As the surviving partner, the widow then became the financial manager for the family.

The close connection between the type of legacy a widow received, where the family lived, and when her husband died can also be seen in a testator's propensity to mention dower or a third (in any context) as well as his inclination to discourage his wife's remarriage (Figure 4-1). Like the bequest of house and supplies, the mention of a third or dower and the penalty for remarriage became less common, particularly in wills probated after 1830. The trends indicate, in addition, that the men of Chester County tended to lag behind Philadelphia residents in abandoning thirds and ceasing to punish remarriage. After 1810, however, this rural difference dissipated as inheritance patterns in both areas generally converged.

Spreading industrialization and an urban-dominated environment probably worked to make a husband less concerned with forms of landed inheritance and more concerned with assisting his family's survival in the rapidly changing economic world around them. In this evolving context, dependence on structured safeguards to protect the children's as well as the wife's portion gave way to reliance on the widow's ability to manage the estate for the benefit of the family. Men made less use of house and supplies legacies because this form of bequest was ill-suited to an increasingly nonagricultural community. Similarly, leaving a widow a traditional third of the estate or restricting her remarriage through economic sanctions hobbled a female head of household who was struggling to prosper in an urban-industrial environment. A man left his wife everything because he expected her, if given the room to maneuver, to weather the storm of economic change. He

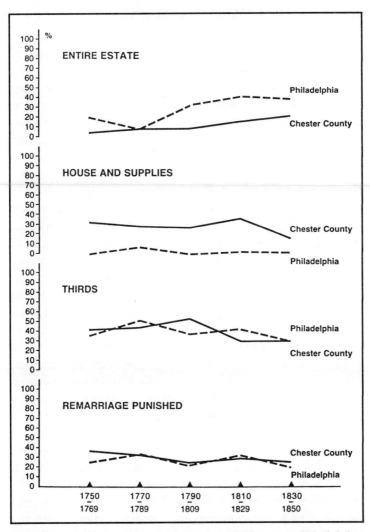

FIGURE 4–1. *Types of Legacies Left to Widows in Philadelphia and Chester County, 1750-1850, as Percentage of All Legacies to Widows* (Sources: Chester County Wills and Administrations, Chester County Archives, West Chester; Philadelphia Wills, Register of Wills, Philadelphia.)

did not want to narrow her options for using her talents and business judgment.

We can trace the economic fate of some widows through probate records, comparing the estates their husbands left them with what they themselves left when they died. The results lend further support to the proposition that a large percentage of women had the economic skills necessary to ensure the economic well-being of their families. This kind of detailed analysis is possible only in Chester County, where the appropriate indexing has been done.[34] The fact that even with a good index only a small number of widows could be traced successfully (65 out of 621) suggests that the majority of women married again, moved, or used a less formal system than probate to bequeath their own goods when the time came.[35] In addition, many women were left property for life only and, therefore, could not legally bequeath their widow's share. Unless they had owned property in trust while married or acquired goods during their widowhood, such women had no property to put through probate. Still, the pattern gleaned from the small group of traceable widows demonstrates the potential for economic gain during widowhood.

Furthermore, widows' inventories show that both those who suffered economic decline and those who prospered did so by substantial margins. Of the 65 women studied, 37 (56.9 percent) lost personal property during their widowhood, while 28 (43.1 percent) increased their personal wealth. The losers experienced a median deficit, corrected for inflation, of $300.71, and the gainers had a surplus of $313.03.[36] These are remarkable changes, given the median inventory values for Chester County widows between 1750 and 1850 (Table 4-5). Some doubled their assets while others, in effect, lost everything.

TABLE 4-5

Median Inventory Values in Dollars for Widows Who Left Wills in Philadelphia and Chester County, 1750–1850

Date	Median Inventory Value ($)	Interquartile Range	Cases
CHESTER COUNTY			
1750–1759	178.98	112.58	5
1760–1769	392.70	611.31	6
1770–1779	386.61	506.84	8
1780–1789	245.07	1,083.48	11
1790–1799	219.37	66.65	4
1800–1809	223.79	1,046.88	6
1810–1819	412.93	887.98	10
1820–1829·	342.93	820.67	6
1830–1839	306.58	1,535.91	9
1840–1850	611.67	2,322.37	9
Total			74
PHILADELPHIA			
1750–1759	437.36	2,046.79	4
1760–1769	1,055.88	2,462.60	5
1770–1779	207.06	583.32	8
1780–1789	339.45	1,281.12	6
1790–1799	713.48	10,883.56	5
1800–1809	207.86	356.00	12
1810–1819	409.04	1,069.46	12
1820–1829	1,044.17	1,749.50	17
1830–1839	319.59	1,181.41	25
1840–1850	1,046.21	3,607.03	30
Total			126

Sources: Chester County Wills and Administrations, Chester County Archives, West Chester; Philadelphia Wills, Register of Wills, Philadelphia.

Note: Values were corrected for Pennsylvania inflation and converted to dollar values, when necessary, according to the procedure outlined in n. 36 to Chapter 4. Only widows with extant inventories are included. The interquartile range is a measure of dispersion calculated by subtracting the first and third quartiles of the inventory values ranked according to size.

That a majority of women died with less personal wealth than their husbands had left them seems to fit in well with the traditional view of limited female financial capability.[37] Some widows may well have lost their inheritances through financial incompetence; given the deference paid to creditors in the Pennsylvania legal system, however, a large part of these losses probably reflected the difference between what a man intended his widow to have and what she actually received once creditors were paid. In addition, it is clear that many widows distributed their personal property before death. In her will, Mary H. Taber, a Philadelphia widow who died in 1849, outlined the money and property she had already given her children. The value of her personal property, according to the inventory taken after her demise, was "$0," with the added notation "given away before death."[38]

It is not surprising that some women dissipated their inheritances; the surprise is that so many women became wealthier. Furthermore, none of the women in this particular sample used remarriage as a strategy for improving their economic position. It is unlikely that fortuitous inheritances or other sudden windfalls account for more than a few instances of improved circumstances. Most women who gained wealth did so by functioning successfully in the male world of business.

In fact, it can be argued that at least some of these economically astute women improved their economic standing precisely because they were *better* entrepreneurs than their husbands. Margaret Holman managed the Yellow Springs Tavern even before her husband's death in 1820. Testimony from the Chester County Orphans Court described her as running the family business with little help from her drunken husband, Frederick.

Before Frederick's death Margaret his wife conducted and managed the business. Frederick did nothing one half of his time. She was industrious, and the manager. She did the money business—even when they lived in the pike—The sons and the girls helped. The sons did the out business for her— and seen to the indoor business. The only gentleman had not been temperate. It preyed on his system and disabled him.

When Frederick died, he left his entire estate to his wife for life. Since she had supported him for years, he probably thought her ably prepared to maintain the business. She soon began to upgrade it with new furniture, bedding, and farming equipment. A former housekeeper at the tavern testified that "the personal property was not valuable when the old man died. It was improved after his death, in Mrs Hs time. I mean by improved that Mrs H got a great many new things and much better." She also "built an addition to the old Manner House," put on a new roof, added "a piassa in front," built another two-story house dubbed "Paradise," and "put up the ten pin alley." Her tavern was valued in 1844 as worth $18,000.[39] She improved both her personal and her real wealth during widowhood by independently managing a successful business.

Other widows excelled in their husbands' traditionally rural business—farming.[40] Catharine Boothe of Penn Township lost her husband, Walter, in 1803. He died intestate, leaving behind forty acres of land worth $800, and $250 worth of personal property. The widow felt that it was her right to take control of the entire estate and try to improve its value. In her will, written in 1834, she described her marital partnership, referring to the few improvements on the farm as the product of "fourteen years of the *united labour* and exertions of *my husband and myself*" and "the personal property *we* had acquired" (italics hers). Left with eight children, ranging in age from four months to thirteen years, she chose to keep farming.

> I concluded not to have the farm sold, for all the property which my husband left If converted into money, (as I then thought and do still think) and divided among the children would in a short time have been consumed by the unavoidable expences of their maintenance & education and they would have been deprived of a home and the means of support. I took the Estate and property as my own and considered and used it as such and have since that time continued to hold occupy and expensively to improve the premises as well by building and lime as in every other way in which the labour of man is requisite. . . . Had I not taken the land in the manner I did as above mentioned it must have brought much less to the children than I now intend they shall be benefited thereby, in this my will.

Her bequests included six tracts of land acquired since her husband's death: a sixteen-acre lot, one of ten to twelve acres, three lots of unspecified size totaling $2,700 in value, and a fifty-acre farm. She died with a personal estate of $3,596.12.[41] This shrewd businesswoman made her family farm a success, yet she could not sign her own name to the will that outlined her achievements.

Involvement in an ostensibly male-owned and male-operated business before or during marriage was an important aspect of a woman's training for the economic challenges of widowhood. As an unpaid partner in a store or a farm, a daughter or wife learned the skills necessary to manage the family operation independently. The death of her father and the absence of her brothers gave Emma M.

Stockton the opportunity to help her mother with the family finances. At twenty-five, she wrote to the family lawyer, William Meredith: "Perhaps you may be surprised at my confidence in writing you, but having been my mothers 'Man of business' for sometime past I have become quite courageous." She questioned Meredith about the sale of a family property that would allow her mother, her sister, and herself to live more comfortably: "It could be sold for $40,000—the debts be paid which I suppose amount to between 7 & $8,000—placing the remainder at Interest, & with the sum remaining of the Lancaster Stock which is but small we would be able to reestablish ourselves & live where we wish."[42] Her mother, Anna, wrote many similarly detailed notes urging Meredith to act on the matter.

> I think that if the Property by being sold at a good price and rested at six percent safely and securely at the same time benefitting my Children it would be much better than leaving it as it is, and paying interest on it, the income from the Property is now $1400, the taxes, interest & repairs take more than half that sum, admitting the Property should clear, *but* *$30,000* we should still have $1800 where we now have 600 or $700 the latter is not sufficient to support us, but at the same time I would be very unwilling to part with it, if I did not believe if would be invested securely and profitably.[43]

The similarity between these two letters shows that the widow and her daughter shared financial information. Emma would start married life with a knowledge of investment strategies learned from her mother.

Among women who chose to establish new businesses rather than follow their husbands' occupations, another female support system emerged. A number of widows left legacies in trust for their married daughters. This practice allowed the daughter to reap the benefit from the invested property independent of her husband's needs or debts and still inherit the entire amount of the trust if widowed. Some women apparently intended this trust to provide their married daughters with the capital to start a business. The widow who left her married daughter money to start a shop probably thought of her bequest as a form of insurance against the marital and financial calamities of widowhood, desertion, and divorce. Jane Allen made no mention of the state of her daughter Mary's marriage in her will, probated in Philadelphia in 1812, but she did give Mary access to her inheritance to open a store. Her legacy was put in trust unless "my said daughter Mary McClintuck should engage in business & should request the said principal & any part thereof to be paid to her to assist her therein."[44] Elizabeth Ming, in her will of 1814, made a similar provision for her daughter, stating specifically that as a widow she might wish to start her own business. The 500 dollars in trust became available to her "should she become a widow and desire to go into any business in which case I authorize the said Trustee to pay her a part or the whole Amt. as she may desire."[45]

With the appropriate skills and capital, widows in Philadelphia and in Chester County sought to maintain or improve their economic circumstances. Yet real differences in the economic aspects of widowhood emerge in the inventories of widows who left wills in one area or the other.[46] (Few widows bothered to construct a will, for approximately the same reasons so many men died intestate.) Philadelphia widows generally died with more personal wealth than their counterparts in Chester County (see Table 4-5). The urban tendency to leave the wife everything accounts for part of the disparity. Indeed, as wives increasingly received their husbands' entire estates in Chester County, and the trend became still more popular among Philadelphia testators, there was a corresponding increase in the value of widows' inventories at the time of their own death.

Local inventory values also reflect the different forms of a widow's wealth in Philadelphia and Chester County. A city dweller acquired more expensive accouterments: A widow who considered herself well-off in Philadelphia might have a carriage and silverplate, while a Chester County widow might consider herself equally prosperous and successful with a functional wagon and more practical pewter. Both women would have the goods necessary for a comfortable existence within their respective communities, but the Philadelphia widow's personal property would be worth considerably more. What even a moderately well-off Chester County widow was likely to have, however, was land and related real property. In the city, in contrast, even the wealthy frequently rented their residences and shops; land is typically missing from urban inventories.

A Philadelphia widow who left a will was also more likely to be *abundantly* wealthy than her rural counterpart. The very richest widows, not surprisingly, lived in the city. In consequence, the range of inventory values for Philadelphia testators was on the whole much greater than that for widowed Chester County testators—mainly the effect of a few very wealthy widows in Philadelphia who left estates worth between $10,000 and $95,000 dollars. No Chester County widow had an inventory worth even $5,000. Economic inequality was a feature of urban life.[47]

In addition to geographic differences, the personal estates of widows in Philadelphia and Chester County show variations over time (Figure 4-2). These fluctuations in the economic climate affected Philadelphia more than rural

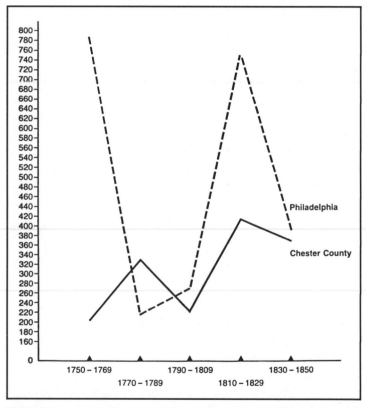

FIGURE 4–2. *Median Inventory Values for Widows Who Left Wills in Philadelphia and Chester County, 1750–1850* (Sources: Chester County Wills and Administrations, Chester County Archives, West Chester; Philadelphia Wills, Register of Wills, Philadelphia.)

Chester County. After 1790, as the regional economy diversified and grew, the rise and fall of Chester County widows' inventory values largely corresponded with those in Philadelphia. Predictably, the personal wealth of widowed testators expanded and contracted along with the economy, although the greater stability of the rural areas shielded residents somewhat from these movements.[48] These urban versus rural patterns were not unique to widows.[49] City life meant financial risk as well as opportunity. After the Revolution, as modern economic growth took hold across southeastern Pennsylvania, widowhood's economic challenges became less linked to the urban or rural character of the environment.

A widow of means took on the role of financial manager for her family, making use of an inheritance appropriate to her circumstances. While some failed, many others succeeded, employing skills acquired during or before marriage. The economically secure widow was free from many of the restrictions limiting the rest of the female population. She had many of the same legal rights as men, and avoided the indignities and restrictions of the charity system. Her success as a "Man of business" illuminates more general female involvement in the male world of work and finance during and after marriage, despite legal restrictions and cultural stereotypes that suggest the contrary.

5

A Death in the Family

As he prepared for death, the typical married man tried to ensure the continuation of a normal life for his family. His widow was expected to maintain the family as a social unit, and other family members were supposed to cooperate in this effort. The family that lost a husband and father survived by subordinating the individual autonomy of its members for the good of the whole. Before death separated them, a thoughtful couple often designed provisions not only to allocate the family resources fairly, but to promote collaboration. The widow and each child would contribute to family stability through arrangements that were often tightly structured. The widow supported, raised, and disciplined her minor children while protecting their property from a potentially unscrupulous second husband. Adult children, whether living in the same house as their widowed mother or not, contributed to the family's welfare by helping to raise the young ones or by participating in the economic life of the household. With a sense of mutuality, the family endured.

Focusing on issues of gender clouds this family perspective; such studies see the widow as depending for her livelihood on her sons or other male kin, with little control over her minor children.[1] In the families studied here, however, mutual obligation and a careful, cooperative use of limited resources governed what happened to a husband's legacy as well as the everyday lives of the widow and her children.[2]

The widow confronted her new circumstances with the indirect help of her deceased spouse. Married men stated in their wills their hopes for family harmony. Ideally, the widow would safeguard the children's interests, and the children would behave properly toward their mother. David Eaton of Chester County expressed this hope in his 1813 testament.

> And it also my will and desire; that all my Children may all live lovingly together; United to Each other & promoting Each Others Welfare. in this life: That they may receive a just Recompence of Reward; in that Life which is to come. But more Especially (it is my will) and dying Request. that all my Children pay a particular regard. and dutiful respect to their dear Mother: by their Conduct. causing her to live as comfortable, as possible in their power: so that her last days. may be her best—AMEN—[3]

Similarly, William Marsh dictated on his deathbed in 1809 the duties required of his eldest son as the main heir: "Son Henry be a son to your Mother, a Brother to your Brother, and a Brother to your Sisters." Each role denoted obligation as well as privilege. A family bereft of a husband and father could continue to function as a unit only with mutual support, shared responsibilities and, perhaps most importantly, affection.

Some men maintained a shadowy presence in the family through provisions designed to continue their parental supervision after death.[4] This posthumous parenting could help the widow to discipline and control the children. William Marsh, for example, warned Henry, "Your Mother is to have what she please and not to be tos,d here and there; but to have what she please."[5] Marsh clearly wanted his son to realize that his economically superior position gave him no right to dictate his mother's share or her living arrangements. A number of married men's wills allowed the widow to vary a child's inheritance according to his or her behavior. David Eaton gave his wife the authority to distribute additional moneys from his personal estate "if in Case any one of my Children should . . . prove more kind: tender. or Affectionate: towards her. in the decline of life. or after my decease."[6] One of the toughest of such provisions was outlined in the 1759 will of Jacob Oberholtrer of Philadelphia.

> It is my will That all my Children shall be Subject & Obedient to their Mother untill they arrive at their full age, And if one of my Children should be disobedient to their Mother, I do then in such Case give full Power & Authority unto her & unto my other Execur. herein after Named to bind Such Child out till yr. same is of full Age.[7]

These men hoped, through a carefully constructed will, to give their widows additional leverage in their difficult role as single parents, and to remain a living force in their families' development.

With an awareness of her husband's legacy to each child, and the use of these disciplinary provisions and the elements of her own will, a widow could shape her children's lives. First of all, the two wills together laid out for each son or daughter an equitable share of the family's assets.[8] A widow using her own last testament to balance the inheritances of her various offspring might carefully mention her affection for all to distinguish this equalizing measure from a disciplinary one. Rebecca Scattergood explained the reduced portion her son's children received in her will of 1800: "It is not a want of love for my deceased son John Scattergood that I have not been more liberal to his children, but on Account of his falling Heir at Law to my late loving Husband."[9] Rebekah Biddle's 1831 will elaborately described her intention to adjust her bequests according to her husband's legacies.

> my said Late husbands Will a large portion of all his Estate is and will be vested in my said Grand Daughter Sarah Biddle Dunlap and in her Mother my said Daughter Ann Dunlap, for which reason and also because I feel an equal degree of affection for all my children. I do hereby dispose of and distribute my Estate and property to and Amongst my other children and Grand children and such other persons as are herein after named and in such manner shares and portions as are herein after mentioned without meaning to convey any idea of a dimmution of the Love and affection for my said daughter Anna Dunlap as for my said Granddaughter Sarah Biddle Dunlap bearing as I have said an equal degree of affection for all my dear children.[10]

The widow complemented her husband's legacies and thereby continued a pattern of parental support that long outlived the original family unit. To maintain the equilibrium of the household, she continued to follow family goals that had been set before the loss of her husband.[11]

Considerations of family survival seem frequently to

have outweighed concern with individual autonomy or
personal power.[12] In some married men's wills, the widow
was restricted from remarriage to protect the property of
minor children from a second husband. But, in a similar
fashion, adult children were required to aid their mother
in settling the estate and supporting the family. When
personal goals were subordinated to family objectives, a
female-headed household could function successfully
without a new patriarch.

A cautious man could also protect the estate of his
minor children by appointing a guardian. Yet most men
who left wills never took advantage of this option, because
it could hinder the widow's ability to respond to new
economic circumstances while doing little to safeguard
the children's property.[13] The exclusion of a widow from
serving as guardian to her own children was not necessarily
a hardship or an indication that her husband considered
her unable to handle the financial duties required of an
early nineteenth-century guardian.[14] Some women actually
refused the post, claiming that the obligations, like those
of executor, were too burdensome. Ann Mendenhall asked
the Chester County Orphans Court to appoint a guardian
for her two sons because she "apprehends ye affaires Will
be much in Cumbring to her."[15] There were also purely
legal reasons for a Pennsylvania widow to be excluded from
the role of guardian. If a widow was the executor of her
husband's estate, according to law she could not act as
guardian of her children's property. And the official ap-
pointment of a guardian probably seemed unnecessary to
some men, because even if a woman remarried she and her
new husband had to post security to protect the children's
legacies.[16] Married male testators apparently avoided the

use of a guardian because this legal mechanism infringed on the autonomy of the family while failing to control the real threat to its security, a new husband and father.

Thus, many testators chose to take away part of their spouses' legacies or limit their control over their children's property *only* if they took a second husband. Mary Eaton received, according to David Eaton's 1813 will, "all my Real. & personal Estate: To hold use occupy & Enjoy with all the proffits arising upon during her state of (Widowhood) or her Natural life if Remaining in that (State)."[17] The intention was to protect the children and the integrity of the remaining family unit,[18] but there was often a hint of hostility toward a wife who would choose to alter that unit through remarriage. The phrasing of many of these provisions actually equated a widow's remarriage with her death in planning the resulting redivision of the family's wealth. Joseph Brinton made clear in his 1752 will that his wife could have her portion only as "a widow on my name."[19] In effect he required that she remain his wife even after his death. Jacob Hipple's 1772 will outlines the effect of remarriage on his wife's portion, in words that reveal his anger at the thought: "If she is to Marry again she is to Clear off the p[l]ace and she is to have nothing of the crop in the grounds."[20] The reversion of a widow's inheritance to her children on remarriage protected the family's assets, but some men were evidently also eager to prevent their wives' from replacing them.

It is impossible to determine whether second husbands commonly misused their power to the disadvantage of the widow and her minor children, but the records show that a widow *could* become the victim of an unscrupulous man. Daniel McKarracher was just such a scoundrel, preying on the lucrative estates of widows and orphaned children. His ruse was outlined in a plea to the Philadelphia Orphans Court in early nineteenth-century Philadelphia:

> In what part of the Universe is their A Man to be found unto who could be So Callous to parental feelings As to banish his own helpless Wife and children from their Native homes in Violation of his Matrimonial Vow, And Afterwards Seduce A widow the Mother of Children, to obtain all she has. And boast he hath in some Years past Accumulated A fortune of four thousand pounds on Orphans Spoils. Gentlemen, Such a Man there is. Who has done all this, And Now is before you, his name is Daniel McKarracher, And we hope their is no other like him—I forbear to descend into particulars, which would make humanity weep and pity bleed. To You Gentlemen I as their Representative Appeal Justice for the Wrongs he has done—He has lived with the Widow for Years past, And has persuaded her to Act with him And do As he says, in fact he keeps her Under fear And Now Assumes An Authority more than a Husband. He has Created himself Landlord And Martin of the Tavern, The profitts Arising from which were very Considerable. More than Sufficient before that to Support the Widow and her children. beside laying up Annually Something handsom but Since he has appropriated all the profitts Arising therefrom to his own Use. he is Collecting in all the Debts that were due to the Deceased. he has Engraved the Intials of his name on the pewter Muggs &c As Landlord. he has the possession of Everything.[21]

This case demonstrates the kind of abuse a widow and her children could suffer at the hands of a second husband, and the public outrage at McKarracher's tyranny over the widow—"An Authority more than a Husband."

A widow with children and other familial responsibilities could protect herself and her dependents from such chicanery with a discreet investigation of her new love interest. A concerned widow and her brother called on Deborah Norris Logan in the spring of 1826 to confirm their suspicions about a certain beau. The widow's brother, leaving his sister in the chaise, asked Mrs. Logan privately if George Farr "had a wife now living?" As a casual acquaintance of Farr's daughter, Elizabeth, Mrs. Logan knew "that his second wife was in being, but that they were separated." The widow was brought into the house to hear the distressing truth.

> She seemed shocked at what I told them I understood to be the case, (but I carefully disclaimed having any knowledge of my own on the subject;) and said she was thankful that she had made the enquiry to save herself—the misery of such an affair—I found by her conversation she was a widow with two children and a mother. to take care of; and a comfortable little property to do it with; to secure which doubtless was the object of George Farr. for the Lady had neither youth nor beauty, nor yet a jaunty air to recommend her. They then declared that what I had told them corroborated so fully what they had heard before as to satisfy them of its truth, and that they would go no further. . . . she understood his wife intended to keep quiet 'till he was again married and then come forward and sue him for a separate maintenance, they took leave.[22]

These are dramatic and blatant examples of the exploitation of a widow and her children. A more likely result of a widow's remarriage would be a subtler neglect of the children's interests. The offspring of a previous marriage were, for both the widow and her new spouse, a constant reminder of a former union. Unhappy memories, jealousy, or a desire to focus on the needs of a new family sometimes resulted in the physical removal of children of the earlier marriage. William Dougherty entered the Philadelphia almshouse at the age of six because his mother's second husband would "not suffer this Child to live with him." His mother wanted him bound out as an apprentice by the almshouse administrators.[23] In a petition to the Philadelphia Orphans Court in 1834, John Cadwalader requested the court to appoint a guardian for his father's young black house servant to prevent the confiscation of the boy's wages.

An orderly well behaved & good boy without any property except his wages which are all required for his maintenance. His father is dead & his mother married again she contributes nothing to his support but demands his wages of his employer & thus prevents this petitioner from receiving the benefit of them.

In response, the court appointed as guardian of the boy "Jesse Hackett who is a very respectable & moral coloured man residing in the same family."[24] Clearly this widow was content with her son's absence from the home and even profited from the arrangement. Like a new husband, the widow herself could exploit a child economically.

In happier circumstances, a stepfather looked after children as if they were his own. Daniel Burkhart married Elizabeth Maag, who at the time of their wedding had eight children and an estate worth about sixteen pounds. When his wife died, Burkhart asked the Philadelphia Orphans Court to allow the three remaining girls, ages eight to fourteen, to stay with him as apprentices. In this way, and with the proper selection of a guardian, this loving stepparent hoped to keep his family together.

> Your Petitioner declares in the Face of God and the World That he always loved these Children in the same degree as if they were his own And that since the death of their Mother her last tenderest Concerns for them have found the way to his own Breast so that if any person under pretence of being the next of kin to their deceased Father or Mother should attempt to persuade or take these Children from him it would give him all the Trouble and Distress which a Father or Mother may feel on the like Occasions.[25]

Some widows clearly remarried for love with the full confidence that their new husbands would protect and care for their children rather than abuse the powers given a husband under Pennsylvania law.

Only a small percentage of married men felt compelled to restict the remarriage of their spouses in their wills. In a sample of married male testators in Philadelphia between 1750 and 1850, just 26.3 percent (75 out of 285) made part of their wives' legacies contingent on continued widowhood. Similarly, 30.2 percent (193 out of 639) of will-writers in Chester County who left widows included such restrictive clauses.[26] This pattern did not simply reflect the percentage of widows left with minor children, since most women had such children when widowed.[27] Nor can we tell from probate records alone whether a widow's youth, beauty, or personality made her a more likely candidate for remarriage.

Yet the presence of children made a difference. A man who was leaving no offspring generally showed less interest in his widow's future matrimonial plans. Among men who died in Philadelphia without mentioning children in their wills, only 13.4 percent (11 out of 82) put marital restrictions on their wives. In Chester County, a slightly larger

20.7 percent (19 out of 92) of childless testators made similar restrictive provisions. Conversely, men with off-spring mentioned marriage restrictions in their wills more often and in about equal proportions in Philadelphia and Chester County: 31.5 percent (64 out of 203) in the city, and 31.8 percent (174 out of 547) in rural Chester. On the whole, a judicious choice of a new spouse became the exclusive concern of the widow when a couple was child-less.

In parallel fashion, men unhampered by a concern for the welfare of their children commonly gave their widows their entire estates without concern about the absorption of their property by a second husband. Among married male testators in Philadelphia without children, 54.9 per-cent (45 out of 82) left everything to their wives. This group differed markedly from married testators with offspring, of whom only 19.2 percent (39 out of 203) left their whole estates to their widows. In Chester County, where this inheritance pattern was generally less common as a result of the agriculturally based economy, 38.0 percent (35 out of 92) of childless testators left their entire estates to their wives,[28] compared with 9.9 percent of men with children (54 out of 547).[29]

The widow without children was also more likely to be appointed sole executor of her husband's estate. The pos-sibility of a remarriage and concern for his children entered into a man's decision to assign a particular person or group to this office. If a widow had executorial duties and remar-ried before her former husband's estate was settled, her new husband often took up these responsibilities. Leaving a widow with minor children as sole executor, therefore, put the children at the mercy of an unknown second husband. In Philadelphia, men with children named their widows sole executor only 11.8 percent of the time (24 out of 203). In contrast, 45.1 percent (37 out of 82) of men without offspring gave their widows' sole executor status. A similar if less pronounced pattern emerges in Chester County, with a mere 7.3 percent (40 out of 547) of men with children, versus 22.8 percent (21 out of 92) of childless men, leaving their spouses to execute the will alone. Concern for the children against determined a widow's treatment in hcr husband's will.

The differences between fathers' wills and those of childless men show that restrictions on remarriage, carefully constructed legacies, and executorial assignments were meant to protect the offspring, not inhibit the options and power of a wife. The survival and well-being of the family, not just an exercise in patriarchal control from beyond the grave, shaped these documents.

The widow and her children likewise took a family-oriented approach to the household's survival. Each member contributed money or services; sometimes family functions such as childcare, food and shelter, and even domestic work were translated into specific monetary terms. Each person had a role within the enterprise.[30]

Anna Stockton, the widow of William Stockton, described to her lawyer, William Meredith, her vision of the family benefits derived from her husband's estate. Among the legacies was a property on Fourth Street in Philadelphia, worth approximately $40,000. The Widow Stockton consulted Meredith about borrowing $10,000 on the property before her husband's affairs were settled. She proposed to lend the money to her son John at 6 percent interest to further his career and promote the position of another son, Philip, who "assisting John in his business . . . is thus freed from many of the dangers of youth." From this arrangement, the Widow Stockton felt, "the family will probably derive much benefit & can sustain no loss." Her plan was designed not only to benefit John but to ensure the whole family's economic success.

> My idea is that such an arrangement would be much preferred to the sale of the 4th Street Property as in the present times it would not bring half its value, & by the arrangement it gives a start to the Boys at the same time secures to the family all the increased value of 4th Street Property that time may give when James will be of age.[31]

This family strategy allowed for both the immediate support and the future economic security of the entire household.

The widow and her children frequently set a value on the services each member rendered to the family. Particularly revealing is the estimate of Rachel Browne, a widow who appeared in Philadelphia Orphans Court in 1805 as the executor of her deceased husband's estate to claim a portion of that estate for childrearing expenses. After collecting and paying debts, the Widow Browne estimated her husband's assets at $4,307.23. She deducted $1,435.74⅓ "as her portion under her Husband will," with the remainder "to be applied to support of Children." She included the following schedule of expenses for the children's "Maintenance": Jno. Browne $225.00, Sarah Browne $415.00, Mary Browne $654.37, Martha Browne $645.00, Joseph Brown $592.95, Henry Brown $537.50. "Ballance advanced for her Children" was $198.33⅓; "Add for Cash advanced for Sarah Brown during her Ilness funeral Expences—& other," $131.00. The total of $3,069.82 exceeded the amount of the estate designated for the children's use by $329.33⅓. Although the court agreed that she had spent more for the children than her husband's estate provided, the justices ruled, "On reference to the Will of said Nathaniel Brown we are of opinion there is nothing due to her from his estate." The strict accounting of monies used for the children's support, and even their funeral expenses, and the "vouchers" the widow kept to verify her claim, demonstrate the acute awareness some families at least had of the proper distribution of family assets.[32]

Ann Mendenhall made a similar request of the Chester County Orphans Court in 1758 to compensate her for her maternal efforts. She felt entitled to be repaid not only for the maintenance of her two sons but for the costs she incurred while giving birth.

> To My Expences Breeding up Moses Mendenhall Son of Caleb Mendenhall from two years & three Months Old till he arived to ye Eage of thirteen years & Six Months Old & Larning him to Read Wright Cypher as far as ye Rule of Fellowship Likewise My Expences of Lying in With Caleb Mendinghall Son of Decd & Breeding him up to ye Eage of Eleven years and Larning him to Read and Right Which Troble & Expense I Submit to ye Judgment of this Honnourable Coart.[33]

Going beyond Rachel Browne, the Widow Mendenhall included services rendered, not just money expended, in her request to the court.

Relations with adult children were often seen in similar financial terms. Mary Pennell, in her 1768 will, gave to her "daughter Hannah Ellis the sum of six pounds to be paid her as *dew* to her for *surveses* don to & for me."[34] In contrast, Catharine Barry, outlining former places of residence for the Overseers of the Philadelphia Almshouse, included her sojourn in Delaware County, where "she went to live on wages with her son George Haskins [for] . . . several years @ 50cts. per week."[35] In both cases money was exchanged for services within the family. Even without the formal, artificial structure of guardianship, a widow and her adult children could still see reciprocal familial services in pecuniary terms.

Under Chester County's poor-relief system, elderly parents often received food and shelter from children in return for a weekly payment.[36] In a case heard by the Chester County Orphans Court in 1838, a witness described such an arrangement:

> I boarded a woman for a year or two for two dollars a week—and I boarded her a while for a dollar a week. She was not in good health when she paid me two dollars a week. . . . She found her own bed & bedding, and her own tea & coffee for herself & her visitors, or I should have charged her more. This woman was my mother in law.—She had a sufficient estate to pay for her keeping. She left about $200, and had an income of about $72 per annum —She willed one hundred dollars of what she had to one of her children—and the other $100 was left to pay her debts and funeral expenses.[37]

This rather cold-blooded account perhaps reflects the disgruntled or mercenary personality of this particular son-in-law. The general significance is that this widow, and presumably others, resided with a daughter and son-in-law, paying for her keep much as widows on outdoor relief paid their caretakers with public funds.

Many households pooled resources to further the financial goals of individual members. Such an informal combination of individual assets could, however, present difficulties if death and the law intervened. Clement S. Miller, who lived with his mother on Third Street in Philadelphia, died in 1843 with his mother's property, as he described the situation to a friend, "mixed up with his own." Miller's widowed parent had lent him stock to "enable him to borrow money for his own use." "He spoke also [to his executor] of the Mortgage of his mothers house in 3d St as having been done for his use." When her son died, the Widow Miller found herself in a legally precarious position, since Clement, although advised by friends to "give his mother a bond and judgment for what he owed her," had neglected to do so.[38] In this case, more careful legal planning would have reinforced and protected the intention of both mother and son to provide for the whole family's welfare by sponsoring gains by one member. When family-focused economic strategies were successful, it was by stressing the viability of the family as a unit and the needs and capabilities of those who composed it.

The life cycle of the family had an impact on the distribution of responsibilities within the household. For example, one would naturally assume that minor children would be a drain on family resources, while adult children would add to the family coffers. Although probate records draw an imperfect portrait of family composition—because they outline legacies, not genealogies—the presence of adult children can be inferred from references to in-laws, grandchildren, and executorial assignments. Among Chester County widows whose economic fate could be traced, the presence of adult children had, if anything, a slightly negative influence on a widow's financial well-being.[39] Among those widows with adult children, 46 percent (17 out of 37) saw their estates increase between the time of their initial inheritance from their husband and their own death. The other 54 percent (20 out of 37) saw their resources decline, despite the fact that they had grown children to help them. Perhaps women were more likely to use their capital to facilitate their children's undertakings in exchange for day-to-day financial assistance. Whatever the reason, adult children cannot be equated with an addition to their mother's resources and minor children with a subtraction: Family strategy suggests a more complex picture of decision making.

The emotional relationship between the widow and her children varied according to the age of the latter. Minor children weighed heavily on a single, widowed parent who had to prepare them for adulthood, whereas grown sons and daughters could aid her in rearing and supporting younger children. Nevertheless, even adult children needed occasional parental reminders of proper behavior as they developed and matured. When a widow lived with her adult children or they lived with her, the thwarted autonomy of both and the uncertain power structure could stress even an apparently harmonious arrangement.

The burden of mothering young children alone fell upon many women. Using data collected by Susan Klepp from Philadelphia church records in the late eighteenth and early nineteenth centuries, it can be estimated that 70 percent (85 out of 121) of women had minor children when widowed.[40] Of this group (widows with at least some minor children), only 20 percent remarried.

For widows blessed with an adequate income, raising young children primarily involved moral instruction and education. Some widows left in comfortable circumstances fretted over the possibility of a decline in status for their

orphaned children, but discipline—particularly of boys—
was a more common concern. Anna Stockton sent her son
William to boarding school, where he soon caused the
headmaster to write about his misconduct.

> Your Son William has been, with other boys guilty of pilfering
> from the garden of one of our neighbors & also of disobeying
> my directions in regard to what had been plundered. The
> conduct is not more repugnant to the laws & orders of the
> Academy than abhorrent to the principles of good morals &
> contrary to the laws under which we live. . . . In these cases
> not only is full restitution to be made to the owners but such
> others censures as the violated laws of the Academy demand,
> must be imposed. To avoid, I suppose the consequences to his
> conduct, William absconded as soon as he found he was
> detected. and has not been seen here this afternoon. I trust
> that arts of larceny are not among the amusements allowed
> him anywhere else, & if they were, the could not be tolerated
> here.[41]

Anna Stockton's reply has not survived, but William surely
incurred her displeasure, if not her anger. Anne Emlen
Mifflin wrote to her mother in 1805 that Lemuel had
charged thirty dollars' worth of clothes, shoes, and station-
ary without his mother's permission. The consequences of
his extravagance were not described.[42] In the correspondence and other records left by widows with young children, daughters were never discussed in a similar context.
Either young boys proved more troublesome than girls, or
widows had less success—or were less sure of themselves—
in disciplining their male children. Widows confronted
many of the same difficulties in raising their children as
did other mothers, but a young man deprived of his father
probably presented a unique challenge.

The first and perhaps overriding concern of the less comfortably situated widow was to feed and clothe her brood. To a woman with a meager inheritance from her husband or a low-paying, marginal occupation, minor children represented a substantial burden. For many, the obligations of rearing children and providing for their economic needs proved overwhelming. Martha Tuft at first relied on her husband's estate to support her six young children, but in 1792, she came before the Philadelphia Orphans Court to request permission to sell land.

> That your Petitioner was left a widow in the year 1788 with six children one of which was, & yet is intirely blind, that with great difficulty she has struggled to maintain & educate them in doing which she has exhausted all the Personal estate of the decd. & the proceeds of two acres of Land in Lancaster County sold by order of the Orphans Court in that County where her husband died, besides contracting some debts which she is anxious to pay & discharge; your Petitioner further states that she is without the means of daily subsistence for herself & children & therefore requests the Authority of this Court to enable her to sell & Convey a Small house & lot of ground situate in Elfrith's Alley in the City Philada. for the purpose of maintaining & Educating her children until such time as they are of age to be placed apprentice.[43]

Six young children drained an otherwise adequate estate, jeopardizing the economic viability of the whole family.

Elizabeth Remington made a similar appeal to the Philadelphia Orphans Court. Her need arose out of difficult economic times. When her husband died in October 1804, the couple had three children, the eldest being five years old. For four years the Widow Remington had "been able by her own exertions to support & maintain the said children." In November 1808, as the American economy responded to the European wars and the embargo on British goods, she found herself, because of "the pressure of the present times . . . unable to . . . [support her children] fully." She asked the justices to allow her to borrow $150 on a $2,200 property, probably a part of the children's legacy from their father, "for the purpose of maintaining the said children and teaching them to read & write &c."[44]

Fortunately, a widow's family often included adult or adolescent as well as minor children. According to Philadelphia church records, the average widow lost her husband at the age of forty-eight after a marriage of twenty-five years.[45] If such a woman conceived in the first five years of her marriage, and death did not take her first-born, she would have adult children when widowed. A widowed mother was more likely to rely upon subtle guidance to mold the actions of an adult child, following patterns of behavior similar to those which Marilyn Ferris Motz has uncovered among elderly mothers and their adult children in nineteenth-century Michigan. Motz's interpretation, however, stresses the mothers' economic helplessness and their limited options in trying to guide their children.[46] Both mothers and fathers were less able to control a grown son or daughter than a young child. The appeal to conscience was developed into a powerful and effective form of discipline.

Without the support of a husband, a mother found her male progeny particularly difficult to control as children and intractable as adults. The complaints against grown sons included irregular letter writing, prolonged absences from home, lack of attention to the family estate, and ill-conceived marriage plans. The tactic most often used to combat these nonconformities was emotional manipulation.

Mary Norris had trouble with her son Isaac, particularly after he left home for a tour of Europe at the age of twenty-three. Once abroad and free of direct parental supervision, the young Isaac began to taste the fruits of independence. He apparently developed a love interest in the spring of 1784, and wrote to inform his sister Deborah of his good fortune. The Widow Norris saw the letter and began to worry that Isaac would marry without her permission. She made her concerns clear in a letter to her errant son, though she expressed confidence in his filial loyalty.

> I entertained a fear, least thee might have formed some plan for fixing in life, before thy return to thy native Country, but thy last to me has dispelled those fears, and I have a Confidence in my dear Child that he will not form any plan for his future life without the knowledge of his affecte. mother, I think thee will comprehend my meaning.[47]

Her efforts to prevent his marriage were apparently successful. Isaac died eighteen years later in 1802, still unmarried at the age of forty-one.

By June of 1784 Mary Norris, perhaps out of concern for his potential matrimonial plans and perhaps to soothe her own loneliness, began to press Isaac to return home. The arguments she used ranged from her ill health to his obligation to care for the family estate.

> I now wish thee to think of returning home, a year has passed since thee left me, let us not be separated another year I intreat thee all thy real friends wish thy return, and I am fully convinced that it will be for thy advantage everyway, as it will

be to me, the greatest consolation to have thee in thy native
Country, & perhaps in attending a little to thy mother, I dont
wish to alarm thy fears, as I know thy affectionate tenderness
to me, but I feel my Constitution (never a strong one) decline
pretty fast.[48]

Isaac, apparently unmoved, forced Mary to switch tactics
in her August letter on the same subject. She now appealed
to mercenary considerations. The Widow Norris found it
cumbersome to care for her son's estate during his absence.
One of his real estate holdings produced no income simply
because it lacked fencing, which made tenants difficult to
procure: "It is a valuable interest and is a pity, it should
remain as it does, if thee was here & managed it thyself I
think thee might manage it to more advantage, then any
attorney could be expected to do."[49] Her plea fell on deaf
ears as Isaac continued his sojourn in Europe.

The widow's displeasure surfaced in familiar terms in
an October 1784 letter in which she lamented to Isaac the
impending departure of her other son, Joseph.

> I hope by this time thee art thinking of returning home by
> next spring, my situation will be lonely indeed, two of my
> Children absent, but I think thy own affairs will require thy
> return, for depende on it, no person can, or will act, in so
> advantageous a manner, as the owner, and was thee here thee
> might put thy Estate in such a Situation as no person can do
> for thee.[50]

Although Isaac eventually returned to Philadelphia, his
alienation from his mother continued, as did her attempts
to mold his behavior. By 1793, nine years after his trip
aboard, Isaac had effectively cut off all ties to his family.

He never wrote to or visited his mother. As Mary Norris informed her daughter in 1795, "poor Isaac I hear seldom of him never from him."[51] (In a 1793 letter to Deborah she had wondered if "he has forgot he has a Mother.")[52] Isaac rebuffed even his brother-in-law, Doctor George Logan.

> But my poor dear Isaac, why will he not come to see me? to see how I live, and how I am settled in all probability for the remainder of my days, he would be a most welcome visitor to me if he chose only to pay me a visit, & if he pleased to continue I could I hope make it agreable to him, provided he would keep within the bounds of moderation, & that would be for his happiness, & well as my Comfort; I am obliged, greatly obliged to Doctr. Logan for calling to see him, & do hope he will not be discouraged by a denial but call again.[53]

The Widow Norris was still trying to influence her thirty-three-year-old son's behavior. Many a widowed mother felt an obligation to do the same. Her tactics changed as her children grew, but the parental role remained an important part of her contribution to the reciprocal set of obligations she saw as essential to the proper functioning of her family.

In parallel fashion, the eldest son of a widow commonly took on a paternal role to help his mother train and discipline his younger brothers and sisters, not just support them financially. A widow turned to a son for help, in particular, with the difficult task of raising the other fatherless boys of the family. He served as an example of proper behavior and as an adviser to the younger children, and took on responsibility for the family if the widow died.

On the eve of a trip abroad, James Craig, the eldest son of Margaret Craig, wrote to his mother from New Castle, Delaware, about his role in the family since his father died in May of the previous year.

It has pleased the almighty Dearest Mother to part us for some time and from present prospects for our mutual Benefit, as it may enable me to return better qualified both in mind and Body to take a fatherly charge of my family—. . . but should it please our father to take you from us my Sister & Brother shall find me a father, Brother & Protector, their interests I here swear shall from that moment be mine more than ever and I hope from the precepts you early instilled into me and my own disposition will give me energy to undertake the task with fervor and delight.[54]

Acutely aware of his new position as male head of the family, he prayed for the strength to shoulder the burden. The death of a father and husband required the family to shuffle and redistribute his various functions.

Grown sons recognized that younger brothers posed particular difficulties for widows. James Craig was especially concerned that his mother refrain from pampering his younger brother. He encouraged her to send young John away to school as soon as possible, after his mother solicited his advice on the subject.

A child of a delicate habit of Body and soft manners should never be brought up among women. . . . mothers are too apt to consider the present more than the future in what are thought trivial matters, but if they would investigate and see the necessity of an entire distinction in the treatment of the two sexes the Generality of mankind would pass their Lives more happily. . . . many would call it Risking too much to expose a tender infant, but I have not the least doubt that where one suffers by neglect there are twenty Ruined by Indulgence & consequent effeminacy.[55]

Whether the well-intentioned widow might in fact jeopardize the masculinity of a young son through overindulgence is of less importance—in the broader context of collective family management—than the perception that she could do so. James Craig apparently felt that his role as eldest male in the family included defining proper gender roles for his young siblings.

Mary Norris wanted her eldest son to counsel and, if necessary, discipline his younger brother. She described her concerns about Charles to Isaac in a letter of 1785. "I am not without my fears in his account he wants Steadiness, and as he professes a greater regard for thee then any one else, I hope thy advice may have weight with him."[56] She pleaded with Isaac to write to his younger brother while abroad, apparently to no avail. A few months later she outlined with need for joint action.

> I feel the want of my eldest Son's, thee my dear I hope may have an influence over Charles, and that influence, with my authority may be absolutely necessary Conduct, I fear he has some acquaintances that are of no use to him; he has been Ill lately, but is now recovered, thee & I must use our best endeavours to fix him (if Wee can) at his outset in life, nobody else will have any influence.[57]

Isaac was expected to take up the role of surrogate father and guide the unruly and free-spirited Charles to a productive adulthood.

Grown sons, in particular, were expected to provide for their widowed mothers, an arrangement that often included sharing the family dwelling.[58] Family leadership, however, involved more than property ownership,[59] and noneconomic interaction did much to shape a family's actual power structure. The standard picture of a long-suffering son reluctantly sharing his home with a widowed mother is too simplistic. For instance, living in the family home, a widow could perceive that she *shared* a dwelling with a son even if the title was in his name. She might see her legacy of various rooms and privileges as a negotiable commodity. The careful partitioning of a house on paper may tell us little about how a hierarchy of property-based power shaped the lives of a bereaved woman and her child within the building. Some widows actually preferred economically inferior living arrangements because these gave them privacy and independence. Sometimes adult children imposed on their mothers by moving in with them.

Clearly, who controlled the *property* in a given household is a poor indicator of who headed the household. Katherine Chew, widow of Benjamin Chew, Jr., inherited the family home under her husband's 1842 will. Although a prolonged legal battle postponed the settlement of the estate, the Widow Chew continued to reside at Cliveden with her eldest living son, Benjamin. Her children on the other side of the legal controversy felt that Ben, Jr., was unfairly claiming that his mother lived in *his* household. Katherine Chew's outraged daughter Eliza referred to Ben's arrogance in a letter to her mother: "He [claimed he] had the command of Clividen from turret to foundation & *you were yourself only a member of his family.*"[60] In this household the widow, although legal owner of the home, was, at least to her son, not the head of the family.

Anna Stockton lived with her son John, but saw the arrangement as part of a network of reciprocal familial obligations that promoted the interests of the whole group. In a letter to her lawyer, William Meredith, in 1836, she described the exchange. She would mortgage the family home for her son's benefit (charging him appropriate interest) and stay in his home with her two daughters: "We will continue to reside with him—*our Company* being sufficient return for favours received."[61]

Even when a widow lived as an apparent dependent in her son's home, occupying certain rooms under her husband's will, the economic power structure could be ambiguous. Jacob Greiner of Philadelphia left his wife one-third of all his property in his 1799 will, but clearly felt that she could reside on her own if she so chose. "I give & bequeath unto my beloved wife Susanna Elizabeth a Bed, Bedstead, & Bedding, one table half dozen windsor chairs, a small tin plate stove, Tea Kettle & Tea apparatus & kitchen furniture sufficient for her to keep House by herself."[62] William Sharples made this alternative explicit in his 1817 will. His wife, Ann, received use of the parlor, an upstairs room, the kitchen, and the cellar, "but if she does not choose to occupy the premise above mentioned she shall not lease or let any other family live therein."[63] This tantalizing will suggests that a widow receiving such a legacy might otherwise have seen her portion of the family home as a piece of property that she could rent out, rather than a required residence. A widow with this option clearly had some say in a household.

At least some legacies designating certain rooms for the widow reflect a desire on the part of the testator to provide his wife with a comfortable and familiar maintenance in her old age. John and Sarah Tyson of Philadelphia obviously lived with their son when John wrote his will in 1775.

I Give and Bequeath to my well beloved Wife Sarah Tyson (if she survives me) the Uninterrupted use of the lower Room or Chamber at the Easterly End of my dwelling house wherein I now dwell (being our now Lodging Room) The Cellar under the same, The new Kitchen which I lately built contiguous to

the same, a priviledge to set up a Bed in the Room Up Stairs
over the first mention Room to lodge her friends Relations or
Acquaintance Occasionally when they may happen to visit
her, And the two Gardens which we now keep for our Use
with free & uninterrupted Ingress Engress & Regress into
upon and out of the said Premises.[64]

Such an arrangement provided elderly parents with retirement care and grew out of concern for an aged spouse, not
from a desire to dictate relations within the household.

Such carefully drawn legacies perhaps reflect the inherent difficulties of sharing a living space. Tamara Hareven
has argued that the widow moved in with her children only
as a last resort—she even preferred boarding strangers in
her home to living with kin.[65] Peter Laslett has similarly
concluded that both the widow and her adult children, if
they had the choice, elected to maintain separate living
quarters in nineteenth-century England.[66] Mother and
child alike sacrificed some degree of privacy and independence when under the same roof. An adult child could also
encounter the added burden of caring for an elderly and
perhaps sick parent. Though potentially a useful mechanism—for both sides—a complex household meant com-
promise and limited independence.

Sharing a home and maintaining some privacy proved
difficult for Margaret Craig and her grown son, James. In a
revealing letter written while abroad in 1808, James discussed the use of lock and key to create a separate space
for himself within the household.

If *you* would stick to the fact and not rush on with accusations
so hastily you would not be subject to the pangs I am now
going to inflict on you—as Henry 4th said at Falstaff, "observe

how a strait story will put you down"—The key of my room that I promised You I gave to Mr Miller with a written direction to deliver it up to you & only you—In that Room were Knox's Essays & the Little poets you talk of, and as for the key of the Tea pot that commands your destiny and the fate of the nation I gave it in charge to William Barclay Hight Esquire to make over to your Ladyship without Delay, knowing that you & aunty B could never spend the summer in peace without rummaging among my affairs.[67]

This son tried to make his room a sanctuary within the family home—with some opposition from his mother. The Widow Craig resented his attempt to close off a part of the house from her, particularly during his prolonged absence from home. The sarcastic tone of this letter clearly demonstrates that their division of living space created some tension.

The care of a sick parent could further complicate such arrangements. Sarak K. Tyson described for the Philadelphia Orphans Court in 1843 the trouble and expense of caring for her terminally ill mother. When Mary Close became very sick, she moved into her daughter's house and soon absorbed all the time and resources of the household. As the owner of a drygoods store, Sarah Tyson used the seamstresses she employed to help nurse her mother and at times had to shut down her business altogether. Her son described the situation to the Orphans Court.

Mrs. Richards, and Mary Kline [seamstresses], nurse and Mother attended several times the store had to be closed and shut up to attend her the business was abandoned at times Mothers business was injured by her attention to grand mother she was preventing making purchases and Sales—She had her hands taken from their business at a great loss to her—I would say this loss amount be at least $150.

Caring for Mary Close involved lifting her in and out of bed and having "the victuals put in her mouth"; "her pillows had to be changed every five minutes," "her friends were entertained there constantly," and "she had to be washed in french Brandy worth $2—a gallon every day two times a day at least." Sarah Tyson asked for $300 from her mother's estate for the expense of constant nursing care, extra housecleaning, and the funeral dinner. The Court awarded the long-suffering daughter $208.[68] The burden of nursing a widowed parent, rather coldly outlined in these legal records, could be considerable.

Aware of this burden, many widows strove to avoid dependence on a grown son or daughter. Some women who had a choice preferred the help of other relatives: Mary Hare, the widowed sister of Elizabeth Powel, turned to her wealthy sibling for help in securing a place of her own. In making the arrangements with her lawyer, Elizabeth Powel explained "that she believed a very oppressive load would be taken off the spirits of my afflicted Sister when she found herself no longer a Burden on the generosity of her Son Charles, and lodged in a House in the vicinity of my Dwelling."[69]

For the widow without wealthy relatives, the almshouse could be preferable to relying on a child's resources. Mary Crawford entered the Philadelphia almshouse in 1811 at the age of seventy: "Since she has lost her Husband, has lived with a Daughter says she understand spinning & woud be glad to be employed."[70] Although her motives remain unclear, the Widow Crawford apparently chose institutional life and the chance of working to support herself over dependence on her daughter.

The laws governing poor relief to some extent encouraged complex household arrangements by requiring family members to support destitute relatives.[71] Support was not always synonymous with shared living quarters.[72] Rebecca Standard, admitted into the Philadelphia almshouse in 1829, had a son living in the city who promised to "pay what he can for her board."[73] Similarly, the grandson of the aged Christiana Sybert agreed with the Overseers of the institution in 1810 to "keep her in clothing & pay her funeral expences in case of death."[74] Yet most widows on public relief in Philadelphia lived in households containing adult children.[75] Some grown children lived with their mothers to stretch their own meager resources. Mary Blackwood had her thirty-two-year-old daughter Jane Clark residing with her, and listed as one of her reasons for needing public funds "children poor."[76] Olive Fullingsby apparently resented the imposition of her thirty-five-year-old son, William, describing him to the Overseers as "poor & good for nothing."[77] Other women lived in a child's home, a burden on an already needy household. Ann Alexander described to the authorities her daughter, Jane—twenty-five-years-old, "marrd with whom she lives"—and gave as a reason for asking for poor relief "daughter poor."[78]

Although the law could force children to support a destitute parent, most widows sought such intervention with diffidence. Mary Sim petitioned the Court of Quarter Sessions in Chester County in 1783 to obtain support from her children only because of her inability to work and only after repeated efforts to persuade them to help her had failed.

Your petitioner . . . by age Sickness and infirmities is Rendered impotent and not able to work, in that your petitioner's

> Children are of Sufficient ability to relieve and Maintain her,
> But have absolutely refused So to do, tho' repeatedly applyed
> to for that purpose, Which has forced your petitioner (tho'
> with great Reluctance) to apply to your Honours, & Humbly
> to Pray that her Children may be compelled by your Honours
> to Relieve and Maintain her, in Such Manner, in Such Manner,
> as your Honours shall direct.[79]

Some women entered the almshouse rather than force their children to comply with the law. The frugal Overseers typically chose to persuade the children of such paupers to fulfill their legal obligation. Elizabeth Tinker, admitted to the Philadelphia almshouse in 1802, "infirm and unable to support herself," was discharged three days later "to her Son Francis Tinker of Southwark labourer (by Order of the visiting Committee) who took her away and promised to provide for *her in future.*"[80]

Mary Beth Norton has argued that daughters were more likely than sons to give emotional aid to a widowed mother, while sons concentrated their help in the financial realm.[81] In the picture presented by these Pennsylvania families, gender lines are not so clearly defined, suggesting that adult daughters and sons provided a combination of emotional and financial assistance.

The particular form of comfort a widow received depended on her own needs. For some, a grown son filled the husband's place better than even the most sympathetic daughter, and emotional dependence on a grown son could be intense. A daughter, nevertheless, could be a helpmate and confidante. Following the loss of her husband, Samuel, in 1740, Sarah Pemberton Rhoads wrote of the support her daughter Mary gave her.

I believe I would have sunk under it, had it not been for the
fortitude, and affectionate attention of this dear child, she
altho' not seventeen years of Age, attended to the Cares of the
family, and interested herself with so much tenderness and
anxiety in my concerns, that I communicated every thing to
her, and derived great reliefe from that confidence, by her
encouraging and Salutary counsel—She would often try to
amuse me, and beg me to exert myself and reflect on what
would be her situation, with that of her young Sister, and
Brother if deprived of my parental Care—She would say—
"Altho' the prospect at present appears gloomy, yet things
may turn out better then thee expects—and if not, do my dear
Mother endeavour to bear it with cheerfulness."[82]

Katherine Chew endured a prolonged separation from
her daughter Anne while the legal battle over her husband's estate split the family. Although she lived with her
grown son, Benjamin, her need for female companionship
and solace went unfulfilled. She wrote to Anne of her
feelings in the fall of 1849.

How hard! how distressing it is, that I can not have *you* with
me to comfort & to soothe me in my trouble! in my desolate
state of widowhood!—Altho' your Brother is kind as possible
to me, yet—Still my poor heart yearns after you!— . . . At
night, when I lay my head on my solitary Pillow my last
Breath is a sigh "Oh my Daughter why are you not with me![83]

A daughter, through her loving companionship, could do
much to help a widowed mother survive the loneliness of
her new circumstances.

The intimacy and interdependence of a widow and her
adult son seems occasionally to have prevented such a
child from starting his own family. Benjamin Chew lived

with his mother until her death and never married. Similarly, James Craig shared a home with his mother until her death and never married. Algernon Logan resided with his widowed mother until his death, also without marrying. Isaac Norris, although unable to live under the same roof with his mother died a bachelor.

The correspondence between James and Margaret Craig contains more than its share of oedipal overtones. While traveling with friends in the fall of 1808, James wrote to his mother constantly and subsequently received some good-natured ribbing from his companions.

> What can you be writing about Craig? Surely there is not enough incidents in this place to furnish a letter every day or two—Some suppose me in Love, and the spleen that the stupidity of this place gives me might be a matter of suspicion—But how very far is it from Being Case, I cannot ever find an individual female that can excite the Least degree of Interest.[84]

James described a companion to his mother in terms that suggest concern about his own indifference to the opposite sex and perhaps a sense that she was responsible for his lack of "energy."

> [He] has more manliness and as much dignity as any man of his age that I ever met with, but too much fire which has constantly been fanned—you should have had the superintendance of his Education and Mrs Smith of mine, not that I want energy in my system but in my manners; tho I do not approve of Boisterosity, firmness & decision are especially necessary in the most severe scenes of life.[85]

This letter was written a few days before James expressed concern about his brother's effeminacy. Less than a month later, James apparently became engaged and then just as quickly broke off the affair. That was as close as he ever came to marrying.

In 1813 Margaret Craig wrote to her niece and confidante with some satisfaction about the domestic arrangement that included mother, daughter, and bachelor son. Although she was superficially supportive, she made it clear that James's marriage was unlikely and (perhaps) unwelcome.

> We should have little of his [James'] company if he were not very domestically inclined, but he is a kind Brother and an excellent son, and never leaves us when he can help it— should you hear of his intended marriage never believe it till I tell you of it—it is talked of every where but without the slightest foundation—the young Lady is a lovely creature & I should have no objection tho' I am not acquainted either with herself or family, but there is nothing but friendship in it nor ever will be—I fear he is not much inclined for matrimony.[86]

The Widow Craig depended on her son to fill a void in the family and step into the roles of father and husband. Her need, combined with James's insecurity, kept this "excellent son" from declaring his independence and starting his own family. The psychological comfort provided by offspring helped the widow to adjust to her loss and the family to continue as an emotionally supportive unit, but for some children the cost was high.

A widow and her children tried together to preserve the family unit through reciprocal obligation and mutual support. Focusing on gender roles obscures the essentially family-centered way in which the widow and her children coped with the death of a husband and father. The death of a married man created a new kind of family—a widow and her orphaned children—who managed as best they could. This meant sacrifices for every family member to promote the good of the whole.

Conclusion

IN 1816 the obituary of "Mary Forbes, widow of William Forbes, merchant, of Philadelphia, aged 84," appeared in a Philadelphia newspaper. Deborah Norris Logan, also a widow, clipped this epitaph and slid it into her diary, noting her sadness at missing the funeral because of bad weather. The Widow Forbes had been a close friend of her mother.

> A woman of rare endowments, exemplary piety and active virtue. For many years she conducted the business of her Husband's compting house with ability, punctuality and dispatch, and was his only clerk: yet was no domestic avocation omitted—her household was always ordered with prudence and economy, and her duties to society, were in no wise neglected. All this was accomplished not by any great effort, but by systematic, unremitted industry, by early rising and by always doing what was to be done at the proper time. . . . Thus in a good old age, with the pleasing recollection of a life well spent, she peaceably sunk into the arms of death, to awake among the immortals, "a new number added to their happy society."[1]

169

This woman's full life included work outside the home in the public sphere, as well as housekeeping and social duties in the private sphere. She carefully balanced these responsibilities to business and family and was admired for her accomplishments. Our understanding of women in early America must have room for such "a life well spent."

The experience of widowed women in late eighteenth- and early nineteenth-century Pennsylvania highlights the need for a reevaluation of the concept of "domesticity," with its presupposition of gender-defined "spheres" and female incompetence in the public domain. This study also suggests that the key lies in a fresh perspective that more fully integrates family and gender issues.

In 1813, Elizabeth Powel described the role of a wife to her nephew, who she feared was contemplating an unwise union.

> The offices of a Wife are very different from those of the mere Pagent of a Ball-room. Something far beyond the elegant Trifler is wanted in a companion for life. She ought to be qualifyed to be the participator of her Husbands cares, the consoler of his sorrows, his stimulator to every precise worthy undertaking, his partner in the vicissitudes of life, the faithful and economical manager, the judicious superintendent of his family, the careful affectionate Mother of his Children, the preserver of his honour, his safe and chief Counsellor.[2]

Though cast in feminine terms, the roles prescribed are those of "partner," "manager," "superintendent," and "counsellor." Female competence and family affection fitted easily together under the rubric of womanhood.

Appendix

AN EXACT count of the widowed population of southeastern Pennsylvania between 1750 and 1850—and of Philadelphia and Chester counties in particular—is not possible with the sources that survive. The federal census became more detailed between 1790 and 1850 but still failed to list marital status or the relation of household members to the designated head of household. An early list of members of the Gloria Dei Church in Philadelphia demonstrates that 56 percent of widowed members in 1754, and 25 percent in 1783/4, lived in homes headed by others.[1] A simple enumeration of women who headed their own households according to census takers would miss this sizable group. The use of life tables and age of marriage is also an unsatisfactory method for estimating the number of widows in the population because of the significant internal migration, particularly among the poorer segments in late eighteenth- and early nineteenth-century America. One glance at almshouse records describing paupers moving from county to county in search of work illustrates the problem. The precise number of widows in the population of either Philadelphia or Chester counties at any particular time, therefore, cannot be determined.

Nevertheless, an early census of Boston gives some clue as to the number of widows in nineteenth-century Philadelphia. The two cities had much in common, including crude death rates.[2] In

1845, Lemuel Shattuck undertook the unusual task of enumerating Boston's population between federal census years because he believed that the 1840 census had underestimated its size. His painfully detailed efforts included the marital status of every inhabitant of the city. According to Shattuck, 9.6 percent of women over fifteen years of age in Boston were widows (3,809 out of 39,666).[3] Using this percentage as a guide, the 41,382 women over fifteen in the 1840 census of Philadelphia probably included 4,000 widows.[4] This rough estimate indicates that widows were a significant group in the population of early Philadelphia.

The characteristics of the widowed population as well as a woman's chances of becoming a widow can be accurately reconstructed using the family reconstitution study done by Susan Klepp for Philadelphia between 1750 and 1830. According to Klepp, married women had a 51 percent chance of experiencing the death of a spouse. The average widow was forty-eight years old at the time of her husband's death.[5] Her marriage had lasted twenty-five years, and she usually remained a widow for thirteen years before she either remarried or died herself. Most (83 percent) never took another husband.[6] In short, widowhood was the fate of many middle-aged women, severing them from a long-time companion and stretching into many years of solitary existence.

Notes

Introduction

1. For an overview of these issues, see Tamara K. Hareven, "American Families in Transition: Historical Perspectives on Change," in *Family in Transition: Rethinking Marriage, Sexuality, Childrearing, and Family Organization*, 4th ed., ed. Arlene S. Skolnick and Jerome H. Skolnick (Boston: Little, Brown and Co., 1983), 73–91.

2. See Appendix.

3. Arlene Scadron, ed., *On Their Own: Widows and Widowhood in the American Southwest, 1848–1939* (Urbana: University of Illinois Press, 1988), 4.

4. For a well-argued treatment of this perspective, see Mary P. Ryan, *Cradle of the Middle Class: The Family in Oneida County, New York, 1790–1865* (Cambridge: Cambridge University Press, 1981); Barbara Welter, "The Cult of True Womanhood," *American Quarterly* 18 (Summer 1966), 151–174.

5. Nancy F. Cott, *The Bonds of Womanhood: "Woman's Sphere" in New England, 1780–1835* (New Haven: Yale University Press, 1977); Carroll Smith-Rosenberg, *Religion and the Rise of the American City: The New York City Mission Movement, 1812–1870* (Ithaca: Cornell University Press, 1971); Carroll Smith-Rosenberg, "The Female World of Love and Ritual: Relations

Between Women in Nineteenth-Century America," *SIGNS* 1 (1975), 1–29; Barbara Berg, *The Remembered Gate: Origins of American Feminism, The Woman and the City, 1800–1860* (New York: Oxford University Press, 1978); Nancy Cott, "Young Women in the Second Great Awakening in New England," *Feminist Studies* 3 (Fall 1975–1976), 15–29; Daniel Scott Smith, "Family Limitation, Sexual Control, and Domestic Feminism in Victorian America," in *Clio's Consciousness Raised,* ed. Mary Hartman and Lois Banner (New York: Harper and Row, 1974), 119–136; Carl N. Degler, *At Odds: Women and the Family in America from the Revolution to the Present* (New York: Oxford University Press, 1980); Ryan, *Cradle of the Middle Class;* Linda K. Kerber, *Women of the Republic: Intellect and Ideology in Revolutionary America* (Chapel Hill: University of North Carolina Press, 1980).

6. Laurel Thatcher Ulrich, *Good Wives: Image and Reality in the Lives of Women in Northern New England, 1650–1750* (New York: Alfred A. Knopf, 1982); Mary Beth Norton, "Eighteenth-Century American Women in Peace and War: The Case of the Loyalists," *William and Mary Quarterly* 33 (1976), 386–409; Mary Beth Norton, *Liberty's Daughters: The Revolutionary Experience of American Women, 1750–1800* (Boston: Little, Brown and Co., 1980), chap. 5; Peggy R. Sanday, "Female Status in the Public Domain," in *Woman, Culture and Society,* ed. Michelle Rosaldo and Louise Lamphere (Stanford: Stanford University Press, 1974), 189–206; Barry Levy, *Quakers and the American Family: British Settlement in the Delaware Valley* (New York: Oxford University Press, 1988), 197–205.

7. Elizabeth Powel to [niece?], n.d., Powel Collection, Historical Society of Pennsylvania, Philadelphia.

8. Linda K. Kerber, "Separate Spheres, Female Worlds, Woman's Place: The Rhetoric of Women's History," *Journal of American History* 1 (1988), 9–39; Lisa Norling, " 'I Have Ever Felt Homeless': Mariners' Wives and the Ideology of Domesticity, 1780–1880," paper presented at the Philadelphia Center for Early American Studies, Philadelphia, 30 October 1987; Michelle Z. Rosaldo, "The Use and Abuse of Anthropology: Reflections on

Feminism and Cross-Cultural Understanding," *SIGNS* 5 (1980), 389–417; Christine Stansell, *City of Women: Sex and Class in New York, 1789–1860* (New York: Alfred A. Knopf, 1986); Ruth M. Alexander, " 'We Are Engaged as a Band of Sisters': Class and Domesticity in the Washingtonian Temperance Movement, 1840–1850," *JAH* 3 (1988), 763–785; Linda K. Kerber et al., "Beyond Roles, Beyond Spheres: Thinking About Gender in the Early Republic," *WMQ* 3 (1989), 565–585; Julie A. Matthaei, *An Economic History of Women in America: Women's Work, the Sexual Division of Labor, and the Development of Capitalism* (New York: Schocken Books, 1982), 124, 133.

9. Elizabeth Powel to John Hare Powel, 16 March 1809, Powel Collection, HSP.

10. Elizabeth Powel to John Hare Powel, 6 January 1811, Powel Collection, HSP.

11. See Gerda Lerner, "The Lady and the Mill Girl: Changes in the Status of Women in the Age of Jackson," *Midcontinent American Studies Journal* 10 (1969), 5–15; Matthaei, *Economic History of Women in America*, 108–116; Kerber, "Separate Spheres," 16–22; Kerber et al., "Beyond Roles," 574–575; Kerber, *Women of the Republic*; Nancy Cott, "Divorce and the Changing Status of Women in Eighteenth-Century Massachusetts," *WMQ* 33 (1976), 586–614; Joan Hoff Wilson, "The Illusion of Change: Women and the American Revolution," in *The American Revolution: Explorations in the History of American Radicalism*, ed. Alfred F. Young (De Kalb: Northern Illinois University Press, 1976), 385–444; Norton, *Liberty's Daughters*; Levy, *Quakers and the American Family*, 21, 193; Gerda Lerner, *The Creation of Patriarchy* (New York: Oxford University Press, 1986).

12. Billy G. Smith, "Death and Life in a Colonial Immigrant City: A Demographic Analysis of Philadelphia," *Journal of Economic History* 37 (1977), 863–889; Sam Bass Warner, Jr., *The Private City: Philadelphia in Three Periods of Its Growth* (Philadelphia: University of Pennsylvania Press, 1968), 51.

13. Warner, *Private City*, 5.

14. Ibid., 57.

15. Ibid., 19.

16. Ibid., 57–61.

17. Ric Northrup, "Decomposition and Reconstitution: A Theoretical and Historical Study of Philadelphia Artisans, 1785–1820" (Ph.D. dissertation, University of North Carolina, Chapel Hill, 1989); Bruce Laurie, *Working People of Philadelphia, 1800–1850* (Philadelphia: Temple University Press, 1980); Sean Wilentz, *Chants Democratic: New York and the Rise of the American Working Class, 1788–1850* (New York: Oxford University Press, 1984); W. J. Rorabaugh, *The Craft Apprentice: From Franklin to the Machine Age in America* (New York: Oxford University Press, 1986).

18. Mary M. Schweitzer, *Custom and Contract: Household, Government, and the Economy in Colonial Pennsylvania* (New York: Columbia University Press, 1987), 21–22.

19. Warner, *Private City*, 9; Billy G. Smith, "Inequality in Late Colonial Philadelphia: A Note on Its Nature and Growth," *WMQ* 41 (1984), 629–645.

20. Thomas M. Doerflinger, *A Vigorous Spirit of Enterprise: Merchants and Economic Development in Revolutionary Philadelphia* (Chapel Hill: University of North Carolina Press, 1986).

21. Gary B. Nash, "Poverty and Poor Relief in Pre-Revolutionary Philadelphia," *WMQ* 1 (1976), 3–30.

22. J. Smith Futhey and Gilbert Cope, *The History of Chester County, Pennsylvania, with Genealogical and Biographical Sketches* (Philadelphia: Louis H. Everts, 1881), 434.

23. James T. Lemon, *The Best Poor Man's Country: A Geographical Study of Early Southeastern Pennsylvania* (New York: W. W. Norton, 1972), 79.

24. James T. Lemon and Gary B. Nash, "The Distribution of Wealth in Eighteenth-Century America: A Century of Change in Chester County, Pennsylvania, 1693–1802," *Journal of Social History* 11 (1968), 7.

25. David E. Dauer, "Colonial Philadelphia's Hinterland Economy: The Wheat Supply System for the Milling Industry,"

paper presented at the Philadelphia Center for Early American Studies, Philadelphia, 20 November 1979.

26. Joan M. Jensen, *Loosening the Bonds: Mid-Atlantic Farm Women, 1750–1850* (New Haven: Yale University Press, 1986), particularly chaps. 5 and 6.

27. Lucy Simler, "Tenancy in Colonial Pennsylvania: The Case of Chester County," *WMQ* 43 (1986), 542–569; Paul G. E. Clemens and Lucy Simler, "Rural Labor and the Farm Household in Chester County, Pennsylvania, 1750–1820," in *Work and Labor in Early America*, ed. Stephen Innes (Chapel Hill: University of North Carolina Press, 1988), 106–143.

28. Schweitzer, *Custom and Contract*, 21–35.

29. Ibid., 87.

30. Lemon and Nash, "Distribution of Wealth," 11–12.

Chapter 1

1. *A Selection of the Letters of the Late Sarah Grubb* (Sudbury: J. Wright, 1858), 439.

2. Deborah Norris Logan Diaries, 2 August 1822, Historical Society of Pennsylvania, Philadelphia.

3. For a description of this process among modern widows, see Arlene Scadron, "Letting Go: Bereavement Among Selected Southwestern Anglo Widows," in *On Their Own: Widows and Widowhood in the American Southwest, 1848–1939*, ed. Arlene Scadron (Urbana: University of Illinois Press, 1988), 246.

4. The sources necessary for understanding how widows viewed themselves unfortunately contain a number of biases. Self-perception can only be approached through personal statements written by the widows themselves in diaries or letters. Individuals who left records tend to have been articulate and wealthier than the average woman. Occasionally, Orphans Court and probate records reveal the widow's thoughts, but these usually lack detail and still represent mostly experiences in the

upper levels of society. Comparison of women's perceptions in Philadelphia and Chester counties is difficult because the bulk of manuscript sources relate to the widowed city-dweller. In spite of all these problems, however, the sources that are available do address some of the core issues that confronted all widows. Not surprisingly, they all dealt with loneliness and despair, and had to adjust to and cope with new responsibilities. The severity of their problems undoubtedly varied from one widow to another, but the challenges were fundamentally similar.

5. David E. Stannard, "Where All Our Steps Are Tending: Death in the American Context," in *A Time to Mourn: Expressions of Grief in Nineteenth Century America*, ed. Martha V. Pike and Janice Gray Armstrong (Stony Brook, N.Y.: The Museums at Stony Brook, 1980), 23–26.

6. Barbara Dodd Hillerman, "Chrysalis of Gloom: Nineteenth Century American Mourning Costume," in Pike and Armstrong, *A Time to Mourn*, 99.

7. Ibid., 101–104.

8. Ibid., 104.

9. *Letters of Sarah Grubb*, 437.

10. Sarah Clayton to Mrs. A. M. Hyson, 28 December 1845, John Clayton Papers, HSP.

11. Helena Znaniecka Lopata, *Women as Widows: Support Systems* (New York: Elsevier, 1979), 129.

12. *Letters of Sarah Grubb*, 437.

13. Logan Diaries, 1 April 1824, HSP.

14. The Buels found a similar emotional pattern in their study of a widowed woman in early Connecticut: Joy Day Buel and Richard Buel, Jr., *The Way of Duty: A Woman and Her Family in Revolutionary America* (New York: W. W. Norton, 1984), 60.

15. Logan Diaries, 1 July 1824, HSP.

16. Logan Diaries, 23 March 1824.

17. Logan Diaries, 9 March 1824.

18. Logan Diaries, 6 March 1824.

19. Logan Diaries, 10 August 1821.

20. Margaret Murphy Craig to Miss Montgomery, 30 September 1809, Biddle–Craig Papers, HSP.

21. Sarah Medford Clayton to John Clayton, 8 December 1840, John Clayton Papers, HSP.

22. Again, this pattern was found by the Buels in Connecticut: Buel and Buel, *The Way of Duty*, 55.

23. Logan Diaries, 2 August 1822, HSP.

24. Margaret Shippen Arnold to Edward Shippen and sisters, 5 October 1802, Burd–Shippen–Hubley Papers, HSP.

25. Logan Diaries, 23 August 1822, HSP.

26. Logan Diaries, 21 July 1825.

27. Margaret Arnold to Edward Shippen, 5 July 1802, Burd–Shippen–Hubley Papers, HSP.

28. Margaret Craig to Nicholas Biddle, 19 February 1811, Biddle–Craig Papers, HSP.

29. Nicholas Biddle to Margaret Craig, 20 February 1811, Biddle–Craig Papers, HSP.

30. Margaret Craig to Nicholas Biddle, 20 March 1811, Biddle–Craig Papers, HSP.

31. Nicholas Biddle to Margaret Craig, 22 March 1811, Biddle–Craig Papers, HSP.

32. Margaret Craig to James Craig, 23 June 1809, Biddle–Craig Papers, HSP.

33. James Craig to Margaret Craig, 6 July 1808, Biddle–Craig Papers, HSP.

34. Sarah Clayton to Mrs. A. M. Hyson, 28 December 1845, John Clayton Papers, HSP.

35. Ibid., 5 May 1847.

36. Logan Diaries, 25 February 1824, HSP.

37. Mrs. Henrietta Lister to Margaret Craig, 23 May 1809, Biddle–Craig Papers, HSP.

38. Margaret Arnold to Edward Shippen, 5 January 1803, Burd–Shippen–Hubley Papers, HSP.

39. *Letters of Sarah Grubb*, 439.

40. Ibid., 437.

41. Logan Diaries, 10 August 1821, HSP.

42. Sarah Clayton to Anna Clayton, 19 June 1846, John Clayton Papers, HSP.

43. Margaret Arnold to Edward Shippen and sisters, 5 October 1802, Burd–Shippen–Hubley Papers, HSP.

44. Logan Diaries, 29 April 1823, HSP.

45. Anne Emlen Mifflin to Ann Emlen, 22 September 1813, Emlen Family Collection, HSP.

46. Sarah Clayton to John Clayton and other children, 31 May 1844, John Clayton Papers, HSP.

47. Sarah Clayton to John Clayton and other children, 19 May 1840, John Clayton Papers, HSP.

48. Logan Diaries, 11 September 1821, HSP.

49. Logan Diaries, 31 May 1826.

50. Logan Diaries, 5 July 1821.

51. Logan Diaries, 8 August 1825.

52. Logan Diaries, 31 May 1826.

53. Mary Bell, Philadelphia Wills (1813), Register of Wills, Philadelphia.

54. Elizabeth Armitt, Philadelphia Wills (1808), RW.

Chapter 2

1. Marylynn Salmon, "Equality or Submersion? Feme Covert Status in Early Pennsylvania," in *Women of America: A History*, ed. Carol Berkin and Mary Beth Norton (Boston: Houghton Mifflin Co., 1979), 92–113; Marylynn Salmon, *Women and the Law of Property in Early America* (Chapel Hill: University of North Carolina Press, 1986).

2. Salmon, *Women and the Law;* Suzanne Lebsock, *The Free Women of Petersburg: Status and Culture in a Southern Town, 1784–1860* (New York: W. W. Norton, 1984); Peggy A. Rabkin, *Fathers to Daughters: The Legal Foundations of Female Emancipation* (Westport, Conn.: Greenwood Press, 1980); Norma Basch, *In The Eyes of the Law: Women, Marriage, and Property in*

Nineteenth-Century New York (Ithaca: Cornell University Press, 1982).

3. For New England parallels, see Douglas Lamar Jones, *Village and Seaport: Migration and Society in Eighteenth-Century Massachusetts* (Hanover, N.H.: University Press of New England, 1981), in particular chap. 6.

4. This sense of limitation is at least implied in many studies of probate data and women's roles. For example, Lois Green Carr and Lorena S. Walsh, "The Planter's Wife: The Experience of White Women in Seventeenth-Century Maryland," *William and Mary Quarterly* 34 (1977), 542–571; Linda E. Speth, "More Than Her 'Thirds': Wives and Widows in Colonial Virginia," in *Women, Family and Community in Colonial America: Two Perspectives*, with an introduction by Carol Berkin (New York: Institute for Research in History/Haworth Press, 1983), 5–41; Lebsock, *Free Women of Petersburg*; Carole Shammas, Marylynn Salmon, and Michel Dahlin, *Inheritance in America from Colonial Times to the Present* (New Brunswick: Rutgers University Press, 1987), 53–54.

5. "An act for the better settling of intestates' estates," *The Statutes at Large of Pennsylvania* (1705/6); "An act for emending the laws relating to the partition and distribution of intestates' estates," ibid. (1748/49); "A supplement to the act, entitled 'An act for the better settling of intestates' estates', and for repealing one other act of general assembly of this province, entitled 'An act for emending the laws relating to the partition and distribution of intestates' estates'," ibid. (1764); "An act directing the dissent of intestates' real estates, and distribution of their personal estates, and for other purposes therein mentioned," *The Statutes at Large of Pennsylvania* (1794); "An Act relating to the descent and distribution of the estates of intestates," in *Digest of the Laws of Pennsylvania*, 7th ed., ed. John Purdon (Philadelphia: Thomas Davis, 1847), 651.

6. Salmon, "Equality or Submersion?" 106–108.

7. William Meredith to Hetty Evans, 1 September 1820, Meredith Papers, Historical Society of Pennsylvania, Philadelphia.

8. Salmon, *Women and the Law,* 147–160.

9. An Act relating to orphans' court," in Purdon, *Digest,* 913.

10. "A supplement to an act, entitled 'An Act relative to . . . secure the rights of married women,'" *Laws of the General Assembly of the State of Pennsylvania* (1848).

11. These figures are based on Jean R. Soderlund, *Quakers and Slavery: A Divided Spirit* (Princeton: Princeton University Press, 1985), appendix B, as well as information kindly provided to me by Dr. Soderlund on individuals who left wills, but whose executors failed to file inventories.

12. Jones, *Village and Seaport,* 88–89; Gloria L. Main, "Probate Records as a Source for Early American History," *WMQ* 32 (1975), 91–98; Daniel Scott Smith, "Underregistration and Bias in Probate Records: An Analysis of Data from Eighteenth-Century Hingham, Massachusetts," *WMQ* 32 (1975), 104; Kenneth A. Lockridge, "A Communication," *WMQ* 25 (1968), 516–517.

13. Shammas et al., *Inheritance in America,* 16. Shammas, Salmon, and Dahlin have found similar testation patterns for early Bucks County, Pennsylvania.

14. Smith, "Underregistration and Bias," 105; Soderlund, *Quakers and Slavery.* According to figures provided by Dr. Soderlund from her study, Philadelphia and Chester County testators (between 1751 and 1780) were wealthier than their intestate counterparts.

15. For a discussion of differences in amount and type of wealth in Chester County and Philadelphia, see Chapter 5 and Sharon V. Salinger and Charles Wetherell, "Wealth and Renting in Revolutionary Philadelphia," *Journal of American History* 71 (1985), 826–840.

16. See Chapter 4.

17. Shammas et al., *Inheritance in America,* 17; Billy Gordon Smith, "Struggles of the 'Lower Sort': The Lives of Philadelphia's Laboring People, 1750 to 1800" (Ph.D. dissertation, University of California at Los Angeles, 1981), 315; David Evan Narrett, "Patterns of Inheritance in Colonial New York City, 1664–1775: A Study in the History of the Family" (Ph.D. dissertation, Cornell

University, 1981), 286; Lebsock, *Free Women of Petersburg*, 38, 53.

18. Mary Beth Norton, "Reflections on Women in the Age of the American Revolution," paper presented at a conference on Women in the Age of the American Revolution, Washington, D.C., 28 March 1985.

19. Katherine Banning Chew, draft of testimony in Orphans Court, 3 April 1848, Chew Family Papers, HSP.

20. Anne Emlen Mifflin, "Acct: of Warner Mifflin, 1799," Emlen Family Collection, HSP.

21. William Griffith, Philadelphia Wills (1841), Register of Wills, Philadelphia.

22. Lebsock, *Free Women of Petersburg*, 58.

23. Salmon, *Women and the Law*, xv.

24. Lebsock, *Free Women of Petersburg*, 67. She does suggest, however, that this passivity changed somewhat over time.

25. Ibid., 76.

26. Marylynn Salmon, "Women and Property in South Carolina: The Evidence from Marriage Settlements, 1730 to 1830," *WMQ* 39 (1982), 680–683.

27. Marriage settlement between Thomas Walker and Hannah Marshall, 18 November 1755, Buffington–Marshall Papers, Chester County Historical Society, West Chester.

28. Marriage settlement between Thomas Cumpston and Eliza M. Crosby, 2 April 1816, Meredith Papers, HSP.

29. Francis Despernay, Philadelphia Wills (1798), RW.

30. Matthias Pennypacker, Chester County Wills and Administrations (1808), Chester County Archives, West Chester.

31. Lebsock, *Free Women of Petersburg*, 77–79.

32. Joan M. Jensen found a similar pattern in *Loosening the Bonds: Mid-Atlantic Farm Women, 1750–1850* (New Haven: Yale University Press, 1986), 24.

33. Sarah P. Howard, Philadelphia Wills (1847), RW.

34. Harriet Thomas, Philadelphia Wills (1845), RW.

35. Margaret Humphreys, Philadelphia Wills (1821), RW.

36. Ann Whittle, Philadelphia Wills (1833), RW.

37. Marylynn Salmon, "Republican Sentiment, Economic Change, and the Rights of Women in American Law, 1780–1820," paper presented at a conference on Women in the Age of the American Revolution, Washington, D.C., 27 March 1985.

38. This analysis is based on a sample of wills probated from 1749/50 through 1850. A 10 percent sample (177 widows and 285 married men) was taken in Philadelphia. Residents of the area outside the modern boundaries of the city (i.e., Montgomery County) were excluded. This western section of Philadelphia County was eliminated from the sample to keep the group primarily urban (if not perfectly so) and yet still include the areas of the county that were part of the urban environment by 1850 though not technically within the city. A 20 percent sample (82 widows and 639 married men) was taken in Chester County because it was expected (incorrectly) that the decedent population there would be smaller. Residents of the eastern area that became Delaware County in 1789 were included.

39. Deborah Norris Logan Diaries, 8 November 1825, HSP.

40. Thomas Hopkinson, Philadelphia Wills (1751), RW.

41. Jackson Turner Main, *Society and Economy in Colonial Connecticut* (Princeton: Princeton University Press, 1985), 44, has uncovered a similar attitude among colonial Connecticut widows.

42. Job Harvey, Philadelphia Wills (1750/1), RW.

43. Aaron Martin, Philadelphia Wills (1829), RW.

44. Abraham Bateman, Chester County Orphans Court (1810), CCA.

45. J. Smith Futhey and Gilbert Cope, *The History of Chester County, Pennsylvania, with Genealogical and Biographical Sketches* (Philadelphia: Louis H. Everts, 1881), 619; James Kelton, Chester County Wills and Administrations (1789), CCA; I would like to thank Laurie Rofini for putting the pieces of this case together for me and bringing it to my attention.

46. Elizabeth Peirsol, Chester County Wills and Administrations (1814), CCA.

47. Samuel Croxson, Chester County Orphans Court (1756), CCA. "Croxton" is the preferred spelling in the documents.

48. Historians often define a widow's power only in formal terms of executorship and restrictions through life estates: see Carr and Walsh, "Planter's Wife," 556–557; Lebsock, *Free Women of Petersburg*, 46; Narrett, "Inheritance in Colonial New York," 142, 171; Speth, "More Than Her 'Thirds'," 18–19; Shammas et al., *Inheritance in America*, 70, 112–119; Deborah Mathias Gough, "A Further Look at Widows in Early Southeastern Pennsylvania," *WMQ* 44 (1987), 829–835. In their view, to have power a widow had to be sole executor of her husband's estate and receive her inheritance in fee simple; a widow who was not an executor, and had her share encumbered with life restrictions, was in a weak position. Suzanne Lebsock has developed an elaborate table to pinpoint the various combinations of executorship, life restrictions, and size of inheritances that widows received. At the top of her "Discretion Spectrum" is the widow who was made sole executor and given her husband's entire estate in fee simple. At the bottom of the scale is the widow whose husband neglected to name an executor and gave her a legacy for life only (*Free Women of Petersburg*, 47). Carole Shammas, in her study of inheritance patterns in Bucks County, Pennsylvania, develops a similar table to describe the "Generosity of Male Testators Toward Their Wives." The highest scores in this generosity index are given to those men who left their wives more than the law allowed, "with no strings attached." Those testators given the lowest scores were ones who bequeathed to their widows less than their legal thirds, and restricted their legacies to widowhood or the children's minority (Shammas et al., *Inheritance in America*, 115). Lebsock, Shammas, and others who have tried to approach the question of female power and the inheritance system consider other aspects of the widow's legacy, but regard executorship and fee simple provisions as the crucial determinants of power.

49. James Kent, *Commentaries on American Law*, vol. 2 (Boston: Little, Brown and Co., 1884), 414–429.

50. Jeremiah Hornketh, Philadelphia Orphans Court (1830), Philadelphia City Archives, Philadelphia.

51. *Account of the Executors of B. Chew's Estate* (n.p.: n.d.), Chew Family Papers, HSP.

52. Benjamin Franklin Bache, Philadelphia Wills (1798), RW.

53. Hannah Pyle, Chester County Orphans Court (1846), CCA; Joseph Pyle, Chester County Wills and Administrations (1844), CCA.

54. This approach was possible in Philadelphia only where the occupation mentioned in a man's will indicated something about his economic position. For the difficulty of making inferences from such occupational labels in Chester County, see Lucy Simler, "Tenancy in Colonial Pennsylvania: The Case of Chester County," *WMQ* 43 (1986), 542–569.

55. Shammas et al., *Inheritance in America,* 54. Shammas found a similar connection between wealthholding and executorial status for widows in colonial Bucks County.

56. Lebsock, *Free Women of Petersburg,* 38. Barry Levy makes a similar argument about Pennsylvania Quakers in *Quakers and the American Family: British Settlement in the Delaware Valley* (New York: Oxford University Press, 1988).

57. Narrett, "Inheritance in Colonial New York." 286.

58. Walter Paxson, Philadelphia Wills (1844), RW.

59. Philadelphia testators who had their wills proved between 1800 and 1850 were examined because during this period the individuals who renounced and who took out letters of testamentary were listed in the will books.

60. Israel Brown, Philadelphia Orphans Court (1805), PCA.

61. Enoch Lloyd, Chester County Wills and Administrations (1775), CCA.

62. John Heilig, Philadelphia Wills (1840), RW. He probably specified a male partner to ensure that his wife's assistant would be free from future coverture restrictions.

63. See Chapter 4.

64. Shammas et al., *Inheritance in America,* 52, 112; Lois Green Carr, "Women and Inheritance in the Colonial Chesa-

peake," paper presented at a conference on Women in the Age of the American Revolution, Washington, D.C., 28 March 1985; Gloria L. Main, "Widows in Rural Massachusetts on the Eve of the American Revolution," paper presented at a conference on Women in the Age of the American Revolution, Washington, D.C., 28 March 1985; David E. Narrett, "Patterns of Inheritance, the Status of Women, and Family Life in Colonial New York," paper presented at a conference on Women in the Age of the American Revolution, Washington, D.C., 28 March 1985; Jensen, *Loosening the Bonds*, 26.

65. Toby L. Ditz, *Property and Kinship: Inheritance in Early Connecticut, 1750–1820* (Princeton: Princeton University Press, 1986), 130.

66. John Hindman, Chester County Wills and Administrations (1802), CCA.

67. Martha Vanderslice, Philadelphia Wills (1761), RW.

68. Mary Beere, Philadelphia Wills (1804), RW.

69. John Dowlin, Chester County Oprhans Court (1849), CCA.

70. Marylynn Salmon, " 'Life, Liberty, and Dower': The Legal Status of Women After the American Revolution," in *Women, War, and Revolution*, ed. Carol R. Berkin and Clara M. Lovett (New York: Holmes and Meier, 1980), 92–94, states that cash was preferable to a life interest in a piece of land. Ditz, *Property and Kinship*, 133–134, disagrees, arguing that a life interest did not strip the widow of all her power.

Chapter 3

1. David Hackett Fischer, *Growing Old in America* (New York: Oxford University Press, 1977), 62; Carole Haber, *Beyond Sixty-Five: The Dilemma of Old Age in America's Past* (Cambridge: Cambridge University Press, 1983), 31; Priscilla Ferguson Clement, *Welfare and the Poor in the Nineteenth-Century City:*

Philadelphia, 1800–1854 (Rutherford, N.J.: Fairleigh Dickinson University Press, 1985), 30; Anne Marie Filiaci, "Raising the Republic: American Women in the Public Sphere, 1750–1850" (Ph.D. dissertation, State University of New York at Buffalo, 1982), 69; Marylynn Salmon, *Women and the Law of Property in Early America* (Chapel Hill: University of North Carolina Press, 1986), 184; Joyce D. Goodfriend, "The Struggle for Survival: Widows in Denver, 1880–1912," in *On Their Own: Widows and Widowhood in the American Southwest, 1848–1939,* ed. Arlene Scadron (Urbana: University of Illinois Press, 1988), 166; Christine Stansell, *City of Women: Sex and Class in New York, 1789–1860* (New York: Alfred A. Knopf, 1986), 12.

2. Examination of the Paupers, 1822–1844, Guardians of the Poor, Philadelphia City Archives, Philadelphia.

3. Ibid. Of the 112 widows examined, 77 named no occupation for their husbands. The occupational categories are drawn from Table 4-4.

4. Examination of Catharine Buckley, Examination of the Paupers, 1831–1839, Guardians of the Poor, PCA.

5. Examination of Margaret Proctor; Examination of Margaret Delany; Examination of Maria Pucé (alias Simmons); all in Examination of the Paupers, 1831–1839, Guardians of the Poor, PCA.

6. Examination of Maria Pucé (alias Simmons), Examination of the Paupers, 1831–1839, Guardians of the Poor, PCA.

7. Admitted Mary Ann Hasty, Daily Occurrence Dockets, 11 December 1828, Guardians of the Poor, PCA.

8. Admitted Mary Craig, Daily Occurrence Dockets, 5 December 1827, ibid.

9. Admitted Rebecca Moore, Daily Occurrence Dockets, 6 October 1792, ibid.

10. William Plumsted and Edward Shippen to Overseers, 29 March 1757, Overseers of the Poor, Society Miscellaneous Collection, Historical Society of Pennsylvania, Philadelphia.

11. For an examination of the marginal nature of women's work in the early nineteenth century, see Jeanne Boydston, "To

Earn Her Daily Bread: Housework and Antebellum Working-Class Subsistence," *Radical History Review* 35 (1986), 7–25.

12. Claudia Goldin, "The Economic Status of Women in the Early Republic: Quantitative Evidence," *Journal of Interdisciplinary History* 16 (1986), 375–404; Carol W. Stevenson, "On Their Own: Widowhood in Nineteenth Century Baltimore," paper presented at the 5th Berkshire Conference on the History of Women, Vassar College, 1981; Susan Grigg, *The Dependent Poor of Newburyport: Studies in Social History, 1800–1830* (Ann Arbor: UMI Research Press, 1984), 102; Mary Beth Norton, *Liberty's Daughters: The Revolutionary Experience of American Women, 1750–1800* (Boston: Little, Brown and Co., 1980), chap. 5.

13. Register of Relief Recipients, 1828–1832, vol. 2, Guardians of the Poor, PCA. This is an alphabetical listing of all outdoor relief recipients. The sample examined here includes all women identifying themselves as widows with last names beginning with the letters A through H. The sample includes 231 widows and 325 cases, since some widows requested aid more than once.

14. Examination of Lavinia Cummells, Examination of the Paupers, 1831–1839, Guardians of the Poor, PCA.

15. Examination of Harriet Ward, Examination of the Paupers, 1839–1844, Guardians of the Poor, PCA.

16. Admitted Elizabeth Ford, Daily Occurrence Dockets, 27 April 1802, Guardians of the Poor, PCA.

17. Admitted Rosannah Davis, Daily Occurrence Dockets, 13 March 1800, Guardians of the Poor, PCA.

18. Billy Gordon Smith, "Struggles of the 'Lower Sort': The Lives of Philadelphia's Laboring People, 1750 to 1800" (Ph.D. dissertation, University of California at Los Angeles, 1981), 300.

19. This characterization of a widow's living arrangements has become the norm in the literature; see Filiaci, "Raising the Republic," 71; Haber, *Beyond Sixty-Five*, 25.

20. A *Census of Pensioners for Revolutionary or Military Services; with Their Names, Ages, and Places of Residence as Returned by the Marshalls of the Several Judicial Districts, Under*

the Act for Taking the Sixth Census (Washington, D.C.: Blair and Rives, 1841).

21. Examination of Hannah Booth, Examination of the Paupers, 1831–1839, Guardians of the Poor, PCA.

22. Register of Relief Recipients, 1814–1815, vol. 1, Guardians of the Poor, PCA.

23. Hannah Bigard, Register of Relief Recipients, vol. 2, 22 December 1828, Guardians of the Poor, PCA; Lydia Branton, ibid., 22 June 1829, Guardians of the Poor, PCA.

24. Within this group I would include the informal aid given by some church groups when approached by a needy widow. Such gifts were rarely recorded in any kind of systematic way, particularly with reference to the marital status of the pauper.

25. Susanna Seyfried, Philadelphia Orphans Court (1801), PCA.

26. Margaret Fullerton, Philadelphia Orphans Court (1791), PCA.

27. Admitted Elizabeth Davis, Daily Occurrence Dockets, 1 May 1802, Guardians of the Poor, PCA.

28. Discharged Susannah Good, Daily Occurrence Dockets, 30 August 1803, Guardians of the Poor, PCA.

29. Sarah Pemberton Rhoads Daybooks, 1796–1798 and 1801–1803, Samuel W. Fisher Daybooks, Samuel W. Fisher Manuscripts, HSP.

30. Admitted Catharine Beale, Daily Occurrence Dockets, 20 March 1800, Guardians of the Poor, PCA.

31. Admitted Margery Olliver, ibid., 26 March 1803, Guardians of the Poor, PCA.

32. Suzanne Lebsock, *The Free Women of Petersburg: Status and Culture in a Southern Town, 1784–1860* (New York: W. W. Norton, 1984), 214; Smith, "Struggles of the 'Lower Sort' "; Gary B. Nash, "Poverty and Poor Relief in Pre-Revolutionary Philadelphia," *William and Mary Quarterly* 1 (1976), 3–30.

33. John K. Alexander, *Render Them Submissive: Responses to Poverty in Philadelphia, 1760–1800* (Amherst: University of

Massachusetts Press, 1980), 123; Lebsock, *Free Women of Petersburg*, 214.

34. Resolution, 31 May 1852, the Indigent Widows' and Single Women's Society, HSP.

35. Clement, *Welfare and the Poor*, 150.

36. Effn[illegible] to Sarah Day, 3 November 1853, the Indigent Widows' and Single Women's Society, HSP.

37. Receipt Book for the Working Committee of the Indigent Widows' and Single Women's Society, 1835, the Indigent Widows' and Single Women's Society, HSP.

38. Extracts from the Minutes, 2 May 1839, the Indigent Widows' and Single Women's Society, HSP.

39. Alexander, *Render Them Submissive*, 123; Carole Haber, "The Old Folks at Home: The Development of Institutionalized Care for the Aged in Nineteenth-Century Philadelphia," *Pennsylvania Magazine of History and Biography* 101 (1977), 240–257; Goodfriend, "The Struggle for Survival," 172.

40. Presbyterian Ministers' Fund, Ledger A, 1761–1798, Presbyterian Ministers' Fund, Philadelphia.

41. For a discussion of the changing federal pension laws, see Constance B. Schulz, "Revolutionary War Pension Applications: A Neglected Source for Social and Family History," *Prologue* 15 (1983), 103–114. And see "An Act for the relief of disabled, aged, and poor revolutionary officers and soldiers," *Laws of the General Assembly of the State of Pennsylvania* (1813).

42. Susannah Jacquet, Philadelphia Orphans Court (1791), PCA.

43. Arlene Scadron in the conclusion of *On Their Own* discusses such "multiple strategies" of survival among more modern widows.

44. Report, 19 February 1842, Chester County Poor House Miscellaneous, Chester County Archives (CCA).

45. Outdoor Allowance Book, 1801–1827 and 1827–1843, CCA. Only seven women were identified specifically as widows in these records.

46. Rebecca Barnard, Outdoor Allowance Book, 27 January 1824, CCA.

47. Betty Chalfant, ibid., 27 May 1828 to 23 October 1838, CCA.

48. Elizabeth Way, ibid., 26 August 1817 to 6 January 1818, CCA.

49. Mary Russel, ibid., 11 May 1819 to 13 September 1824, CCA.

50. Alexander, *Render Them Submissive*, 9.

51. Nash, "Poverty and Poor Relief," 28.

52. Clement, *Welfare and the Poor*, 70.

53. Register of Relief Recipients, vol. 1, 1814–1815, Guardians of the Poor, PCA. This calculation includes all women who were listed as widows in the comments section of this list, 231 in all.

54. Grigg, *Dependent Poor of Newburyport*, 118 n. 1. Joyce D. Goodfriend noted a similar pattern for a later period in "The Struggle for Survival," 182.

55. Alexander, *Render Them Submissive*, 91; Clement, *Welfare and the Poor*, chap. 3.

56. Ann Eliza Weston, Examination of the Paupers, 1839–1844, Guardians of the Poor, PCA.

57. Clement, *Welfare and the Poor*, 70.

58. Hannah Campbell, Register of Relief Recipients, 7 December 1832, Guardians of the Poor, PCA.

59. Susan Carbon, Register of Relief Recipients, 31 January 1829, Guardians of the Poor, PCA.

60. Elizabeth Brotherton, Register of Relief Recipients, 21 December 1829, Guardians of the Poor, PCA. The most bizarre-sounding reason given for requesting the aid of the Guardians was that of Mary Feeble, who at age fifty-six was "confined to bed with open legs": Mary Feeble, Register of Relief Recipients, 19 October 1829, Guardians of the Poor, PCA.

61. Ann Clark, ibid., 5 January 1829, Guardians of the Poor, PCA.

62. Mary Curry, ibid., 10 August 1829, Guardians of the Poor, PCA.

63. J. Smith Futhey and Gilbert Cope, *The History of Chester County, Pennsylvania, with Genealogical and Biographical Sketches* (Philadelphia: Louis H. Everts, 1881), 403–405.

64. Nash, "Poverty and Poor Relief," 5–16.

65. Clement, *Welfare and the Poor*, 83.

66. Ibid., 178–179.

67. Ibid., 93.

68. Alexander, *Render Them Submissive*, 87.

69. Clement, *Welfare and the Poor*, 178–179.

70. References to the Philadelphia Almshouse population of widows are based on a study of all women calling themselves widows recorded between 1789 and 1834 in the Daily Occurrence Dockets, Guardians of the Poor, PCA. This population includes 1,948 widows and 2,256 cases, since some women entered more than once. These records begin in 1789 and go up through the nineteenth century, with gaps in 1791 and 1794.

71. Arlene Scadron describes a similar ruse among the present-day divorced, who sometimes report to the census taker that they are widowed; *On Their Own*, 308.

72. See, for example, "An Act relating to the support and employment of the poor," *Laws of the General Assembly of the State of Pennsylvania* (1836).

73. Examination of Mary Nannium, Admissions and Examinations Book, 31 May 1844, CCA; Directors Chester County to Directors Delaware County, ibid., 20 September 1841, CCA; Directors Chester County to Directors Delaware County, ibid., 15 May 1844, CCA. This woman appears as both Mary Nannium and Mary Nannum.

74. Admitted Fatnel, Daily Occurrence Dockets, 27 September 1796, Guardians of the Poor, PCA.

75. Admitted Ann Lowry, ibid., 19 March 1801, Guardians of the Poor, PCA.

76. Admitted Anna Shaffer, ibid., 5 February 1800, Guardians of the Poor, PCA.

77. Admitted Sarah Renny, ibid., 7 December 1830, Guardians of the Poor, PCA.

78. Admitted Maria Miller, ibid., 26 March 1829, Guardians of the Poor, PCA.

79. Admitted Rebecca Jenkins, ibid., 24 July 1821, Guardians of the Poor, PCA.

80. Admitted Maria Brack, ibid., 1 March 1819, Guardians of the Poor, PCA.

81. Admitted Mary Allen, ibid., 1789–1790, Guardians of the Poor, PCA; Admitted Mary Keating, ibid., 30 November 1802, Guardians of the Poor, PCA; Admitted Jane Ann Smith, ibid., 18 May 1801, Guardians of the Poor, PCA.

82. Admitted Lydia Shippler, ibid., 9 February 1820, Guardians of the Poor, PCA.

83. Admitted Mary Beesley, ibid., 21 September 1804, Guardians of the Poor, PCA.

84. Some 71.1 percent, so far as can be estimated from the records.

85. This estimate was derived from the number of widows who entered the almshouse between 1812 and 1834 (Daily Occurrence Docket, Guardians of the Poor, PCA) as a percentage of the female population in the institution (Alms House Weekly Census, Guardians of the Poor, PCA).

86. Clement, *Welfare and the Poor*, 75.

87. Alexander, *Render Them Submissive*; Smith, "Struggles of the 'Lower Sort' "; and Clement, *Welfare and the Poor*, have all found similar seasonal patterns.

88. Report, Chester County Poor House Miscellaneous Records, 19 February 1842, CCA.

89. Admitted Ann Kyle, Daily Occurrence Dockets, 17 December 1831, Guardians of the Poor, PCA.

90. Grigg, *Dependent Poor of Newburyport*, 48.

91. Admitted Mary Allen, Daily Occurrence Dockets, 1 September 1800, Guardians of the Poor, PCA.

92. Admitted Catharine Blight, ibid., 1 June 1801, Guardians of the Poor, PCA.

93. Eloped Catharine Blight, ibid., 8 July 1801, Guardians of the Poor, PCA.

94. Admitted Betsy Curry, ibid., 1 October 1832, Guardians of the Poor, PCA.

95. Black Women in the Women's Lunatic Asylum, Statistics of Almshouse 1837, HSP.

96. For a discussion of the 1837 census of the black population of Philadelphia as well as the occupations of black women, see Theodore Hershberg, "Free Blacks in Antebellum Philadelphia," in *The Peoples of Philadelphia: A History of Ethnic Groups and Lower-Class Life, 1790–1940*, ed. Allen F. Davis and Mark H. Haller (Philadelphia: Temple University Press, 1973), 111–133.

97. Alice Kessler-Harris, *Out to Work: A History of Wage-Earning Women in the United States* (New York: Oxford University Press, 1982), 27; Alexander Keyssar, "Widowhood in Eighteenth-Century Massachusetts: A Problem in the History of the Family," *Perspectives in American History* 8 (1974), 98–99; Douglas C. North, *The Economic Growth of the United States, 1790–1860* (New York: W. W. Norton, 1966), 170.

Chapter 4

1. To make this analysis, it is necessary to know something of the resources and experiences of the women involved at the time they lost their husbands. Categorizing by class or socioeconomic status, however, is more difficult for women than for men. For one thing, many of the conventional measures used to determine "class" for groups of men are inappropriate for groups of women. Male-oriented occupational divisions, for instance, tend to disregard women who worked in the home or held marginal jobs. For wives and young, unmarried daughters, perhaps the status of a husband or father can serve as a rough measure of their own standing in society. It is virtually impossible, however, to establish historically familiar class divisions—particularly detailed rankings of wealth—for adult women without a male provider. For very few women do adequate direct data on property

and related particulars exist. Nevertheless, wills, letters and diaries, in spite of their well-known inherent social and educational biases in favor of the upper class, can reasonably be said to give some useful insight into the economic circumstances of middling or wealthy widows. See Gloria L. Main, "Probate Records as a Source for Early American History," *William and Mary Quarterly* 32 (1975), 96; Daniel Scott Smith, "Underregistration and Bias in Probate Records: An Analysis of Data from Eighteenth-Century Hingham, Massachusetts," *WMQ* 32 (1975), 105; Alice Hanson Jones, "Wealth Estimates for the American Middle Colonies, 1774," *Economic Development and Cultural Change* 18 (July 1970), 108. To some extent at least, women's wealth can be identified more directly through the use of tax records, census data, and accounts of administration filed in Orphans Court. The papers of this court provide specific information about some estates (testate and intestate) and will be exploited when possible. On the whole, the widows examined in this chapter are from the middle and upper tiers of early Mid-Atlantic society.

2. Marylynn Salmon, "Equality or Submersion? Feme Covert Status in Early Pennsylvania," in *Women of America: A History*, ed. Carol Berkin and Mary Beth Norton (Boston: Houghton Mifflin Co., 1979), 106–108.

3. Carole Shammas, Marylynn Salmon, and Michel Dahlin, *Inheritance in America from Colonial Times to the Present* (New Brunswick: Rutgers University Press, 1987), 52 (they argue, however, that the generosity of Bucks County testators toward their wives was mitigated by the restrictions put on the use of these bequests); Linda E. Speth, "More Than Her 'Thirds': Wives and Widows in Colonial Virginia," in *Women, Family and Community in Colonial America: Two Perspectives*, with an introduction by Carol Berkin (New York: Institute for Research in History/ Haworth Press, 1983), 105; Alexander Keyssar, "Widowhood in Eighteenth-Century Massachusetts: A Problem in the History of the Family," *Perspectives in American History* 8 (1974), 83–119.

4. Katherine Banning Chew to Anne Sophia Penn Chew, n.d.,

Chew Family Papers, Historical Society of Pennsylvania, Philadelphia.

5. James Gibb, Chester County Orphans Court (1780), Chester County Archives, West Chester.

6. "A Supplement To an act, entitled 'An act relative to . . . secure the rights of married women,'" *Laws of the General Assembly of the State of Pennsylvania* (1848). This act gave all women the right to own their own property and write a will, indirectly providing some relief for widows, who became less dependent on their husbands' legacies for their economic survival. The law governing inheritance, although restated in various ways, changed little with regard to the widow's share up to this point. See "An Act for the better settling of intestates' estates," *The Statutes at Large of Pennsylvania* (1705/6); "An act for emending the laws relating to the partition and distribution of intestates' estates," *The Statutes at Large of Pennsylvania* (1748/9); "A supplement to the act, entitled 'An act for the better settling of intestates' estates,' and for repealing one other act of the general assembly of this province, entitled 'An act for emending the laws relating to the partition and distribution of intestates' estates,'" *The Statutes at Large of Pennsylvania* (1764); "An act directing the descent of intestates' real estates, and distribution of their personal estates, and for other purposes therein mentioned," *The Statutes at Large of Pennsylvania* (1794); "An Act relating to the descent and distribution of the estates of intestates," *Laws of the General Assembly of the State of Pennsylvania* (1832–1833). For other discussions of the lag between social and legal change in relation to the Married Women's Property Acts, see Norma Basch, *In the Eyes of the Law: Women, Marriage, and Property in Nineteenth-Century New York* (Ithaca: Cornell University Press, 1982), or Peggy A. Rabkin, *Fathers to Daughters: The Legal Foundations of Female Emancipation* (Westport, Conn.: Greenwood Press, 1980).

7. For a description of the probate sample discussed, see n. 38 to Chapter 2.

8. Lucy Simler, "The Union of Manufacturing and Agricul-

ture in Colonial Pennsylvania," paper presented at the annual meeting of the Organization of American Historians, New York, 13 April 1986; Lucy Simler, "Tenancy in Colonial Pennsylvania: The Case of Chester County," *WMQ* 43 (1986), 542–569; Paul G. E. Clemens and Lucy Simler, "Rural Labor and the Farm Household in Chester County, Pennsylvania, 1750–1820," in *Work and Labor in Early America*, ed. Stephen Innes (Chapel Hill: University of North Carolina Press, 1988), 106–143.

9. Richard Downing, Chester County Wills and Administrations (1820), CCA.

10. Frederick Dallman, Philadelphia Wills (1793), Register of Wills, Philadelphia.

11. Shammas et al., *Inheritance in America*, 53–58; James T. Lemon, *The Best Poor Man's Country: A Geographical Study of Early Southeastern Pennsylvania* (New York: W. W. Norton, 1972); James A. Henretta, "Families and Farms: *Mentalité* in Pre-Industrial America," *WMQ* 35 (1978), 3–32; Keyssar, "Widowhood," 83–119; Philip Greven, *Four Generations: Population, Land, and Family in Colonial Andover, Massachusetts* (Ithaca: Cornell University Press, 1970); John J. Waters, "Patrimony, Succession, and Social Stability: Guilford, Connecticut, in the Eighteenth Century," *Perspectives in American History* 10 (1976), 131–160; Carole Haber, *Beyond Sixty-Five: The Dilemma of Old Age in America's Past* (Cambridge: Cambridge University Press, 1983), 20–22; Mary P. Ryan, *Cradle of the Middle Class: The Family in Oneida County, New York, 1790–1865* (Cambridge: Cambridge University Press, 1981), 29–30.

12. At least since the appearance of Richard Hofstadter's, *The Age of Reform: From Bryan to F.D.R.* (New York: Alfred A. Knopf, 1955), historians have been aware of the dual role of the farm as a business enterprise and an integral part of the lineal family. A controversy in which James Lemon *(Best Poor Man's)* and James Henretta ("Families and Farms," 3–32) have been especially active stems from a false dichotomy. As Hofstadter suggested a generation ago, entrepreneurial orientation and family values cannot in fact be separated when examining the family farm. The present

analysis offers a similar interpretation of economic interest, family strategy, and ideology for other kinds of family businesses as well.

13. George Smedley, Chester County Wills and Administrations (1765), CCA.

14. Leonard Walker, Chester County Wills and Administrations (1825), CCA.

15. Simler, "Tenancy in Colonial Pennsylvania," 542–569.

16. John Dicky, Chester County Wills and Administrations (1797), CCA.

17. Bettye Hobbs Pruitt, "Self-Sufficiency and the Agricultural Economy of Eighteenth-Century Massachusetts," WMQ 41 (1984), 348.

18. Lemon, Best Poor Man's, 155.

19. Pruitt, "Self-Sufficiency," 343–344.

20. Shammas, et al., Inheritance in America, 53, 112–113, have found that house and supplies provisions for widows in rural Bucks County, Pennsylvania, slowly declined from the eighteenth to the nineteenth centuries.

21. James K. Somerville sees a similar pattern in eighteenth-century Salem, Massachusetts, which he connects also to broader socioeconomic trends: see "The Salem (Mass.) Woman in the Home, 1660–1770," Eighteenth-Century Life 1 (September 1974), 11–14.

22. Joan M. Jensen also observed this in her study, Loosening the Bonds: Mid-Atlantic Farm Women, 1750–1850 (New Haven: Yale University Press, 1986), 26.

23. Lisa Wilson Waciega, "Reply to Deborah Mathias Gough, 'A Further Look at Widows in Early Pennsylvania,'" WMQ 44 (1987), 837–839.

24. Claudia Goldin, "The Economic Status of Women in the Early Republic: Quantitative Evidence," Journal of Interdisciplinary History 16 (1986), 381–382 and table 5.

25. Jeanne Boydston, "To Earn Her Daily Bread: Housework and Antebellum Working-Class Subsistence," Radical History Review 35 (1986), 16; Christine Stansell, City of Women: Sex and

Class in New York, 1789–1860 (New York: Alfred A. Knopf, 1986), 11.

26. Thomas Bryan, Philadelphia Wills (1799), RW.

27. John Stroup, Philadelphia Wills (1825), RW.

28. Elizabeth Powel to Thomas Pichands, 23 May 1811, Powel Collection, HSP.

29. E. Powel to John Hare Powel, 16 March 1809, Powel Collection, HSP.

30. Mary Norris to Isaac Norris, 8 April 1785, Norris Family Letters, HSP.

31. M. Norris to Deborah Norris Logan, 17 March 1795, Maria Dickinson Logan Family Papers, HSP.

32. E. Powel to J. H. Powel, 6 January 1811, Powel Collection, HSP.

33. E. Powel to John Elliot Cresson, 12 August 1811, Powel Collection, HSP.

34. Bart Anderson et al., comps., *Index to Chester County, Pennsylvania Wills and Intestate Records, 1713–1850* (Danboro, Pa.: Richard P. and Mildred C. Williams, 1970). This index is an alphabetical listing of both testate and intestate individuals, listing place of residence and date. Philadelphia has a more cumbersome index based on an alphabetical listing by date. To use this index for tracing a name without knowing a specific date requires a tedious examination of all listings under the first letter of the person's last name.

35. The number 621 includes both the widows who left wills and named their deceased spouses and men who left widows and mentioned them by name. Since the Chester County index to wills and administrations stops in 1850, the widows of men who died toward the end of this period could not be traced.

36. These dollar values were constructed from the wholesale price indexes in Anne Bezanson et al., *Wholesale Price in Philadelphia: 1784–1861* (Philadelphia: University of Pennsylvania Press, 1936), 390–391, table 40; and Anne Bezanson et al., *Price and Inflation During the American Revolution: Pennsylvania, 1770–1790* (Philadelphia: University of Pennsylvania Press, 1951),

343, table 2. These two tables were made compatible using the average monthly prices between 1741 and 1745 as a base. The conversion rate used by Bezanson is seven shillings sixpence in Pennsylvania currency per dollar. Dollars became the standard currency used in inventory evaluations around 1810.

37. Mary Beth Norton, "Eighteenth-Century American Women in Peace and War: The Case of the Loyalists," *WMQ* 33 (1976), 386–409; Barry Levy, *Quakers and the American Family: British Settlement in the Delaware Valley* (New York: Oxford University Press, 1988), 197–205.

38. Mary H. Taber, Philadelphia Wills (1849), RW.

39. Frederick Holman, Chester County Orphans Court (1841), CCA.

40. For another example of a successful farming widow in Chester County, see Jensen, *Loosening the Bonds*, chap. 8.

41. Catharine Boothe, Chester County Wills and Administrations (1846), CCA.

42. Emma Stockton to William Meredith, September 1836, Meredith Papers, HSP.

43. Anna Stockton to William Meredith, 5 April 1836, Meredith Papers, HSP.

44. Jane Allen, Philadelphia Wills (1812), RW.

45. Elizabeth Ming, Philadelphia Wills (1814), RW.

46. See n. 38 to Chapter 2. The inventory values in this section have been standardized over time using the procedure outlined in n. 36 above. Inventory values in Pennsylvania reflect an individual's personal, not real, wealth. Occasionally wills mention real estate, but not often or consistently enough to permit a complete analysis of real wealth.

47. Gary B. Nash, *The Urban Crucible: Social Change, Political Consciousness, and the Origins of the American Revolution* (Cambridge: Harvard University Press, 1979); Billy G. Smith, "Inequality in Late Colonial Philadelphia: A Note on Its Nature and Growth," *WMQ* 41 (1984), 629–645.

48. These fluctuations are presented with the prices controlled for inflation as outlined in n. 36 above.

49. The work that has been done on inventory values for men includes either both testate and intestate individuals or deals only with the eighteenth century: Nash, *Urban Crucible;* Lemon, *Best Poor Man's;* Duane Eugene Ball, "The Process of Settlement in Eighteenth-Century Chester County, Pennsylvania: A Social and Economic History" (Ph.D. dissertation, University of Pennsylvania, 1973).

Chapter 5

1. James T. Lemon, *The Best Poor Man's Country: A Geographical Study of Early Southeastern Pennsylvania* (New York: W. W. Norton Co., 1972); James A. Henretta, "Families and Farms: Mentalité In Pre-Industrial America," *William and Mary Quarterly* 35 (1978), 22; Alexander Keyssar, "Widowhood in Eighteenth-Century Massachusetts: A Problem in the History of the Family," *Perspectives in American History* 8 (1974), 83–119; Philip Greven, *Four Generations: Population, Land, and Family in Colonial Andover, Massachusetts* (Ithaca: Cornell University Press, 1970); John J. Waters, "Patrimony, Succession, and Social Stability: Guilford, Connecticut, in the Eighteenth Century," *Perspectives in American History* 10 (1976), 131–160; Carole Haber, *Beyond Sixty-Five: The Dilemma of Old Age in America's Past* (Cambridge: Cambridge University Press, 1983); Mary P. Ryan, *Cradle of the Middle-Class: The Family in Oneida County, New York, 1790–1865* (Cambridge: Cambridge University Press, 1981), 28–30; Carole Shammas, Marylynn Salmon, and Michel Dahlin, *Inheritance in America from Colonial Times to the Present* (New Brunswick: Rutgers University Press, 1987).

2. Henretta, "Families and Farms," 28–29; Gail S. Terry, "Women, Property, and Authority in Colonial Baltimore County, Maryland: Evidence from the Probate Records, 1660–1759," presented at a conference on The Colonial Experience: The Eighteenth-Century Chesapeake, Baltimore, Maryland, 13–15 Sep-

tember 1984; Tamara K. Hareven, "Family Time and Historical Time," *Daedalus* 106 (Spring 1977), 64–65. These works similarly acknowledge the importance of reciprocity in family functioning.

3. David Eaton, Chester County Wills and Administrations (1813), Chester County Archives, West Chester.

4. Lorena S. Walsh found a similar pattern among seventeenth-century Marylanders; see her " 'Till Death Us Do Part': Marriage and Family in Seventeenth-Century Maryland," in *The Chesapeake in the Seventeenth Century: Essays on Anglo-American Society*, ed. Thad W. Tate and David L. Ammerman (Chapel Hill: University of North Carolina Press, 1979), 136–137.

5. William Marsh, Chester County Wills and Administrations (1809), CCA.

6. David Eaton, Chester County Wills and Administrations (1813), CCA.

7. Jacob Oberholtrer, Philadelphia Wills (1759), Register of Wills, Philadelphia.

8. David Evan Narrett noted this practice in colonial New York City; see his "Patterns of Inheritance in Colonial New York City, 1664–1775: A Study in the History of the Family" (Ph.D. dissertation, Cornell University, 1981), 219.

9. Rebecca Scattergood, Philadelphia Wills (1800), RW.

10. Rebekah Biddle, Philadelphia Wills (1831), RW.

11. Compare Joel T. Rosenthal, "Aristocratic Widows in Fifteenth-Century England," in *Women and the Structure of Society: Selected Research from the Fifth Berkshire Conference on the History of Women*, ed. Barbara J. Harris and JoAnn K. McNamara (Durham, N.C.: Duke University Press, 1984). In a related argument, Rosenthal makes the point that widows die at a later point in the lifecycle of the family than their former husbands. This determines the outline of their wills. The husband on his death had more young children to launch in the world. His widow, on the other hand, had fewer unsettled children and more grandchildren who received token legacies of affection.

12. Unlike Henretta, who stresses lineage rather than family survival ("Families and Farms," 28–29), Terry hints at the joint

familial outlook of husband and wife ("Women, Property and Authority").

13. For a discussion of the probate sample on which this analysis is based, see n. 38 to Chapter 2.

14. Suzanne Lebsock, *The Free Women of Petersburg: Status and Culture in a Southern Town, 1784–1860* (New York: W. W. Norton Co., 1984), 40–42; Michael Grossberg, *Governing the Hearth: Law and the Family in Nineteenth-Century America* (Chapel Hill: University of North Carolina Press, 1985), 242–253; Barry Levy, *Quakers and the American Family: British Settlement in the Delaware Valley* (New York: Oxford University Press, 1988), 201–205.

15. Caleb Mendenhall, Chester County Orphans Court (1758), CCA.

16. "An Act relating to Orphans' Court," *Laws of the General Assembly of the State of Pennsylvania* (1832).

17. David Eaton, Chester County Wills and Administrations (1813), CCA.

18. Linda E. Speth, "More Than Her 'Thirds': Wives and Widows in Colonial Virginia," in *Women, Family and Community in Colonial America: Two Perspectives*, with an introduction by Carol Berkin (New York: Institute for Research in History/Haworth Press, 1983), 20; Roger Craige Henderson, "Community Development and the Revolutionary Transition in Eighteenth Century Lancaster County, Pennsylvania" (Ph.D. dissertation, State University of New York at Binghamton, 1982), 156; David E. Narrett, "Patterns of Inheritance, the Status of Women, and Family Life in Colonial New York," paper presented at a conference on Women in the Age of the American Revolution, Washington, D.C., 28 March 1985.

19. Joseph Brinton, Chester County Wills and Administrations (1752), CCA.

20. Jacob Hipple, Chester County Wills and Administrations (1772), CCA.

21. Daniel McKarraher, c. 1794–1816, folders 2 and 8, Box 122, Meredith Papers, Historical Society of Pennsylvania, Phila-

delphia. Both "McKarraher" and "McKarracher" are used in the documents consulted.

22. Deborah Norris Logan Diaries, 3 March 1826, HSP.

23. William Dougherty, Daily Occurrence Dockets, 18 May 1804, Guardians of the Poor, Philadelphia City Archives, Philadelphia.

24. Theodore Quaintin, Philadelphia Orphans Court (1834), PCA.

25. Daniel Burkhart, Philadelphia Orphans Court (1773), PCA.

26. See Figure 4-1.

27. Haber, *Beyond Sixty-Five*, 10. This statement is also based on information provided to me by Susan Klepp from her study of church records in Philadelphia. See Susan Edith Klepp, "Philadelphia in Transition: A Demographic History of the City and Its Occupational Groups, 1720–1830" (Ph.D. dissertation, University of Pennsylvania, 1980).

28. See Chapter 4.

29. Other historians have found similar patterns in Pennsylvania and other colonies: Billy Gordon Smith, "Struggles of the 'Lower Sort': The Lives of Philadelphia's Laboring People, 1750 to 1800" (Ph.D. dissertation, University of California at Los Angeles, 1981), 306; Gloria L. Main, "Widows in Rural Massachusetts on the Eve of the American Revolution," paper presented at a conference on Women in the Age of the American Revolution, Washington, D.C., 28 March 1985; Narrett, "Patterns of Inheritance," 177–179; Lois Green Carr and Lorena S. Walsh, "The Planter's Wife: The Experience of White Women in Seventeenth-Century Maryland," *WMQ* 34 (1977), 555–556.

30. Christine Stansell makes a similar argument for New York; however, she sees hierarchies even within such a family structure: *City of Women: Sex and Class in New York, 1789–1860* (New York: Alfred A. Knopf, 1986), 52.

31. Anna Stockton to William Meredith, 16 September 1834, Meredith Papers, HSP.

32. Rachel Browne, Philadelphia Orphans Court (1805), PCA.

33. Caleb Mendenhall, Chester County Orphans Court (1758), CCA.

34. Mary Pennell, Chester County Wills and Administrations (1768), CCA.

35. Examination of Catharine Barry, Examination of the Paupers, 1839–1844, Guardians of the Poor, PCA.

36. See Chapter 3.

37. Alexander Strawbridge, Chester County Orphans Court (1838), CCA.

38. Clement S. Miller, Philadelphia Orphans Court (1843), PCA.

39. For an explanation of this group and the price indexing used to calculate these values, see nn. 35 and 36 to Chapter 4.

40. See n. 27 above.

41. W. R. Johnson to Anna Stockton, n.d., Meredith Papers, HSP.

42. Anne Emlen Mifflin to Mother, 10 October 1805, Emlen Family Collection, HSP.

43. Martha Tuft, Philadelphia Orphans Court (1792), PCA.

44. Elizabeth Remington, Philadelphia Orphans Court (1808), PCA.

45. Information supplied by Susan Klepp; see n. 27 above.

46. Marilyn Ferris Motz, *True Sisterhood: Michigan Women and Their Kin, 1820–1920* (Albany: State University of New York Press, 1983), 68.

47. Mary Norris to Isaac Norris, 15 May 1784, Norris Family Letters, HSP.

48. Mary Norris to Isaac Norris, 17 June 1784, Norris Family Letters, HSP.

49. Mary Norris to Isaac Norris, 7 August 1784, Norris Family Letters, HSP.

50. Mary Norris to Isaac Norris, 30 October 1784, Norris Family Letters, HSP.

51. Mary Norris to Deborah Norris Logan, 17 March 1795, Maria Dickinson Logan Family Papers, HSP.

52. Mary Norris to Deborah Norris Logan, 29 July 1793, Norris Family Letters, HSP.

53. Mary Norris to Deborah Norris Logan, 15 March 1793, Maria Dickinson Logan Family Papers, HSP.

54. James Craig to Margaret Craig, 1808?, Biddle–Craig Papers, HSP.

55. James Craig to Margaret Craig, 3 August 1808, Biddle–Craig Papers, HSP.

56. Mary Norris to Isaac Norris, 9 September 1785, Norris Family Letters, HSP.

57. Mary Norris to Isaac Norris, 29 December 1785, Norris Family Letters, HSP.

58. Lemon, *Best Poor Man's*; Henretta, "Families and Farms"; Keyssar, "Widowhood"; Greven, *Four Generations*; Waters, "Patrimony, Succession and Social Stability"; Haber, *Beyond Sixty-Five*; Ryan, *Cradle of the Middle Class*.

59. Nevertheless, many historians rely on the census, tax lists, and other documents based on property ownership to analyze family interaction and power: Peter Laslett, *Family Life and Illicit Love in Earlier Generations: Essays in Historical Sociology* (Cambridge: Cambridge University Press, 1977), 198; Ryan, *Cradle of the Middle Class*, 192.

60. Eliza Chew Murray Mason to Katherine Banning Chew, 6 November 1845, Chew Family Papers, HSP.

61. Anna Stockton to William Meredith, 2 February 1836, Meredith Papers, HSP; compare Joy Day Buel and Richard Buel, Jr., *The Way of Duty: A Woman and Her Family in Revolutionary America* (New York: W. W. Norton, 1984), 226. In this study of a colonial Connecticut woman, the Buels found that she too considered herself a useful addition to a grown child's household, not a burden.

62. Jacob Greiner, Philadelphia Wills (1799), RW.

63. William Sharples, Chester County Wills and Administrations (1817), CCA.

64. John Tyson, Philadelphia Wills (1775), RW.

65. Hareven, "Family Time," 65.

66. Laslett, *Family Life and Illicit Love*, 212–213.

67. James Craig to Margaret Craig, 6 July 1808, Biddle–Craig Papers, HSP.

68. Mary Close, Philadelphia Orphans Court (1843), PCA.

69. Elizabeth Powel to George Harrison, 18 September 1813, Powel Collection, HSP.

70. Admitted Mary Crawford, Daily Occurrence Dockets, 28 November 1811, Guardians of the Poor, PCA.

71. See, for example, "An Act relating to the support and employment of the poor," *Laws of the General Assembly of the State of Pennsylvania* (1836).

72. Peter Laslett makes this point about the English poor law in *Family Life and Illicit Love*, 179.

73. Admitted Rebecca Standard, Daily Occurrence Dockets, 4 June 1829, Guardians of the Poor, PCA.

74. Admitted Christiana Sybert, Daily Occurrence Dockets, 19 December 1810, Guardians of the Poor, PCA.

75. See n. 13 to Chapter 3 for a description of the sample of widows taken from the Register of Relief Recipients, 1828–1832.

76. Mary Blackwood, Register of Relief Recipients, 8 August 1829, Guardians of the Poor, PCA.

77. Olive Fullingsby, Register of Relief Recipients, 29 June 1829, Guardians of the Poor, PCA.

78. Ann Alexander, Register of Relief Recipients, 8 August 1829, Guardians of the Poor, PCA.

79. Mary Sim's Petition, Chester County Quarter Sessions Court (1783), CCA.

80. Admitted Elizabeth Tinker, Daily Occurrence Dockets, 26 January 1802, Guardians of the Poor, PCA.

81. Mary Beth Norton, *Liberty's Daughters: The Revolutionary Experience of American Women, 1750–1800* (Boston: Little, Brown and Co., 1980), 97.

82. Sarah Rhoads, "Some account of my beloved daughter," 1796–1801, Samuel W. Fisher Manuscripts, HSP.

83. Katherine Chew to Anne Chew, 29 October 1849, Chew Family Collection, HSP.

84. James Craig to Margaret Craig, 2 August 1808, Biddle–Craig Papers, HSP.

85. James Craig to Margaret Craig, 28 July 1808, Biddle–Craig Papers, HSP.

86. Margaret Craig to Miss Montgomery, 16 November 1813, Biddle–Craig Papers, HSP.

Conclusion

1. Newspaper clipping in Deborah Norris Logan Diaries, 22 February 1816, Historical Society of Pennsylvania, Philadelphia.

2. Memorandum, 13 April 1813, Powel Collection, HSP.

Appendix

1. C. J. Stillé, *Archivum Americum: Upsal Documents Relating to the Swedish Churches on the Delaware*, vol. 1 (Philadelphia: Historical Society of Pennsylvania, 1891), 493–514; Gloria Dei Church (MSs. by E. D. McMahon, 1924), vol. 1, Genealogical Society of Pennsylvania, Philadelphia, 755–772. For a discussion of the nature of this material see Susan Klepp, "Five Early Censuses," *Pennsylvania Magazine of History and Biography* 106 (1982), 483–514. I would like to thank Susan Klepp for sharing her work with me and providing me with a list of widows in these records.

2. Comparisons of crude death rates between Boston and Philadelphia were provided to me by Susan Klepp from the "Reports of Committee on Meteorology and Epidemics of the College of Physicians of Philadelphia," *Transactions of the College of Physicians of Philadelphia* 1 (1846), 33–36, 115–119, 195–204, 270–279, 402–415, and from Lemuel Shattuck, *Report of the Committee of the City Council Appointed to Obtain the Census of Boston for the Year 1845* (Boston: John H. Eastbern, 1846), 130.

Many authors have made comparisons between these two cities, most notably Gary B. Nash, *The Urban Crucible: Social Change, Political Consciousness, and the Origins of the American Revolution* (Cambridge: Harvard University Press, 1979).

3. Shattuck, *Report of the Committee,* 62.

4. *Sixth Census or Enumeration of the Inhabitants of the U.S. as Corrected at the Department of State, in 1840* (Washington, D.C.: Printed by Blair and Rives, 1841), 150–152.

5. Most women were over thirty-six when widowed.

6. Susan Edith Klepp, "Philadelphia in Transition: A Demographic History of the City and Its Occupational Groups, 1720–1830" (Ph.D. dissertation, University of Pennsylvania, 1980). These data were gleaned with much patience from Susan's original notes one long Saturday afternoon.

Index

211

AMERICAN CIVILIZATION

A series edited by Allen F. Davis